The Firm and Territory

This book investigates the relationship between the firm and the territory, emphasizing the micro-organizational dimension and the interactions between actors at territorial levels.

First, the book examines the particular features of the firm considering three key factors – structural design, power configuration and organizational culture – and the characteristics of the surrounding territory as a specific spatial ecosystem with its own institutions, agents, history and objectives. Second, it analyses organizational tenets at the micro- and meso levels with a view to explaining various relational models and their implications at the level of the firm and the territory. Although previous studies have focused on the territory as a geographical space in which firms procure resources and promote development, this book presents an innovative approach and makes a key contribution to the literature by dealing with the firm and the territory from an organizational perspective.

The relationship is analysed as bidirectional: a key question concerns how the territory can impact the organizational dimension of the firm, and how the firm can characterize the territory. This will be considered in connection with various effects. The positive effects of the relationship with the territory are investigated in terms of territorial identity, territorial resilience and territorial sustainability. The negative effects include the role of criminal networks rooted in the territory, with firms acting as key agents.

Roberta Troisi is an Associate Professor and the Director of the Observatory for Territorial Development in the Department of Political and Communication Science at the University of Salerno, Italy.

The Firm and Territory
An Organizational Perspective

Roberta Troisi

Routledge
Taylor & Francis Group
LONDON AND NEW YORK

G. Giappichelli Editore

First published 2023
by Informa Law from Routledge
4 Park Square, Milton Park, Abingdon, Oxon OX14 4RN

and by Informa Law from Routledge
605 Third Avenue, New York, NY 10158

Informa Law from Routledge is an imprint of the Taylor & Francis Group, an informa business

British Library Cataloguing-in-Publication Data
A catalogue record for this book is available from the British Library

Library of Congress Cataloging-in-Publication Data
Names: Troisi, Roberta, author.
Title: The firm and territory : an organizational perspective / Roberta Troisi.
Description: Abingdon, Oxon ; New York, NY : Routledge, 2023. | Series: Routledge-Giappichelli studies in business and management | Includes bibliographical references and index.
Identifiers: LCCN 2022038457 (print) | LCCN 2022038458 (ebook) | ISBN 9781032429595 (hardback) | ISBN 9781032429618 (paperback) | ISBN 9781003365075 (ebook)
Subjects: LCSH: Industrial organization (Economic theory) | Economic geography.
Classification: LCC HD2326 .T76 2023 (print) | LCC HD2326 (ebook) | DDC 338.6--dc23/eng/20220923
LC record available at https://lccn.loc.gov/2022038457
LC ebook record available at https://lccn.loc.gov/2022038458

ISBN: 978-1-032-42959-5 (hbk)
ISBN: 978-1-032-42961-8 (pbk)
ISBN: 978-1-003-36507-5 (ebk)

DOI: 10.4324/9781003365075

Typeset in Sabon
by MPS Limited, Dehradun

To Paolo

Contents

List of figures and tables

Figures

Tables

Introduction: The organizational perspective and its importance in characterizing the relationship between the firm and the territory

This introduction outlines the aims of the study, focusing on the advantages of the organizational perspective in relation to the existing literature. It examines the gaps in the literature in terms of the relationship between firms and the territory, and then outlines the theoretical framework and its added value. Finally, this chapter lists the key research questions, showing how they are addressed in the remaining chapters of the book.

The relationship between the firm and the territory is the focus of the present study. This is not a new research topic. On the contrary, there is an extensive literature that considers this relationship to be key to understanding a series of economic processes that resist the logic of globalization, opposing large-scale standardization, while highlighting and promoting distinctive features and capabilities at territorial level. In various ways, clusters, industrial districts and the concept of ecosystems account for local economic dimensions capable of standing up against the standardization of the world of business. However, the concept outlined here focuses on the territory in a different way, less commonly used in management studies and more closely related to a branch of geographical studies in which the territory is characterized in terms of its autonomy rather than simply in terms of the diversity of its geographical location compared to other geographical locations.

The concept of the territory under consideration here is a unit of analysis that is independent from firms since it is made up of a network of relationships. It is a series of economic and socio-cultural relationships, including those with firms or individual firms. This concept places the territory at the centre of the discussion, considering it as an intelligent container, an accumulator (Malmberg et al., 1996) of resources, particularly knowledge, endowed with a wealth of specific resources (Capello, 2019). The territory comes prior to but does not exist solely due to the presence of firms and actors legitimizing it. Rather, it is the outcome of co-creation over time due to the interaction between natural and human resources, relating to the ways in which resources are exploited, tensions and conflicts are managed, and people coexist. The territory is thus a relational space (Lussault, 2007) rather than simply a context (Baccarani et al, 2019),

DOI: 10.4324/9781003365075-1

and its development is dependent on established communities (Simone & Barile, 2016; Simone et al., 2015). Territorial actions consist of heterogeneous processes (natural, social, technical and economic), in the same way as the actors are heterogeneous. Each process contains the territory and at the same time is contained in the territory.

This framework allows for an innovative interpretation of the relationship between the firm and the territory. The relationship is bidirectional: it can be broken down into the actions of individual agents, but it does not always produce virtuous outcomes. The environment influences decisions, strategies and the behaviour of firms, and vice versa. Firms have the ability to influence the territory, either directly by shaping local behaviour or indirectly as a result of its actions at territorial level. The implications are not always positive. Due to the characteristics it possesses, the link between the firm and the territory can result in a virtuous process but also pave the way for wrongdoing. Territorial characteristics may give rise to "competitive advantages" that are neutral in terms of their contingent use. In addition, since the dimension investigated is consists of relationships, the firm can be taken as the main unit of analysis, emphasizing the micro features, while analysing the firm within a network, emphasizing the meso features.

What is the significance of the organizational approach in this investigation?

This approach is primarily motivated by two factors. The first concerns the way relations are shaped, based on organizational dimensions: the firm uses the resources available to cultivate and manage such relations. In this study, the key dimensions in which the firm cultivates relations and is rooted in the territory are power, structure and culture. Firms exercise power or may be subject to the power of territorial actors. The local culture influences the firm, while the corporate culture can have an impact on the territory. In addition, the firm cultivates relations through its own structure, which may be modified to meet the needs of the territory. The second factor includes the organizational framework in an analysis of the relations. It provides not only an understanding of the organizational dimension but also of the circumstances under which this dimension can be adapted. Essentially, an attempt is made to explain the "what" and the "why", using the resources available to the organization.

Arguably, studies prior to this analysis have tended to investigate the features that characterize the firm, mostly those with a positive impact on the territory. Many studies have examined the positive implications, and the means required for these positive impacts to be enhanced and made permanent. This includes issues such as local development, sustainability and so on. The approach we propose allows us to bring these perspectives together by establishing a more active contact between firms and the territory. It enables us to examine firms by focusing on the micro and meso dimensions, as well as the implications within and beyond the firm. Arguments drawn from the theoretical frameworks of the organizational literature are used to support this approach.

As a result, the research questions seek to address these issues. First, under what conditions does the firm engage in activities with territorial implications and why? Second, what organizational dimensions does the firm use? Third, are the outcomes of this activity positive or negative? Fourth, is mutual influence possible? In other words, how does the territory influence business decisions through a network of agents?

Issues such as sustainability, territorial identity and resilience may be examined in the same way as issues such as corruption and illegal land use by firms. The argument that this analysis wishes to put forward is straightforward, but hopefully worthy of further consideration. Due to the distinct capabilities of the relation between the firm and the territory, opportunities and threats are a matter of speculation. Understanding the causes, mechanisms and effects gives rise to the need to determine appropriate measures in this field. The defence against aggressive globalization processes, the recognition of the value of the capacities of the territory and the firm that increase their chances of survival, is of paramount importance. There is a potential for negative action within this relationship that can be turned into something that is beneficial, efficient and stable. This is the distinction that needs to be the focus of our research.

1 Key features of the relationship between the firm and the territory

1.1 The territory as a spatial system of relations

This study provides an in-depth examination of the relationship between the firm and the territory. Clearly, this relationship has been the subject of previous studies. The number of papers on this topic has increased exponentially in recent years (Zimmermann, 2001; Gonçalves et al., 2011; Baccarani et al., 2019).

The innovative aspect of this study is the idea that this relationship should be examined in depth based on two specific concepts, the first of which entails an idea that is not highly developed in relation to the territory. This is a concept imported from economic geography (Maskell, 2001; Sternberg, 2021; Nicotra et al., 2018), close to the notion of entrepreneurial ecosystems (Cavallo et al., 2019; Stam & Van de Ven, 2021), but with its own specific characteristics. The fundamental idea is that the confines of the territory are determined by a set of relations consisting of connections to the firm for various reasons, not necessarily legitimate, that may be formal or informal, with the firm either subject to or exerting influence. This leads on to a consideration of the second innovative aspect of this study. Although interpersonal relations are the key elements of these reflections, the organizational approach may be used as a theoretical perspective to examine the circumstances in which the firm relies on a series of relations to develop a strong territorial identity. It will be argued that there is a need to understand the organizational aspects that are exploited for the construction of territorial relations, and to characterize them in a theoretical framework.

As a result, it is essential to take the territory as a conceptual starting point. In this study, it is described as a particular form of entrepreneurial ecosystem, of which it replicates many characteristics while being characterized by a series of further features, some of which need to be the focus of an analytical study.

Both of these aspects share the notion of complexity that can be expressed in terms of the interaction among heterogeneous actors operating within a given environment, and at the same time, between these actors and the environment (Sassi et al., 2019; Cochrane, 2018). Based on this idea,

DOI: 10.4324/9781003365075-2

the system is complex because it is both human and natural, with implications for the processes and models of investigation (Ostrom, 2009; Preiser et al., 2018).

Looking more specifically at entrepreneurial ecosystems, they are considered as a series of characteristics, for the most part positive, together with a series of actors, for the most part promoting development, supporting firms in their specific environments.

Moreover, in many cases, the unit of analysis is not the individual firm but rather a network of firms that taken together are capable of benefitting from the advantages offered by a specific geographic area in terms of growth and innovation (Spigel, 2017; O'Connor et al., 2018).

Local cultural orientations, social networks, human capital, economic policies and higher education institutions contribute to environments that are conducive to innovation, sustainability and resilience on the part of firms, depending on the cases considered (Acs et al., 2014; Feldman et al., 2005). More specifically, ecosystems are often characterized by the presence of family firms, a diversified economy, the strong presence of company infrastructures, the availability of investment capital, a widespread entrepreneurial culture along with policies conducive to the setting up of companies at local level (Kuckertz, 2019).

Essentially, ecosystems represent a powerful conceptual construct that can accommodate a range of perspectives, all of which are linked to the idea that these systems, properly understood and exploited, can provide an important competitive advantage for firms. However, there is a limit in this framework that is closely linked to the idea of the ecosystem. The system as a whole exists only from a strictly entrepreneurial point of view, carrying out the economic function of maximizing the performance of the firm (section 1.2) that is thus not only active but also positive. Firms benefit from ecosystems, and this benefit is perfectly legal (Motoyama & Watkins, 2014). The opposite is not necessarily the case, and as a result studies that take into account the capacity of the firm to influence factors beyond the confines of the firm are limited in number, and tend to consider just one aspect of the ecosystem, usually the cultural aspect. Moreover, since the function of the ecosystem, broadly speaking, is to maximize the potential of the firm, it may be taken for granted that the ecosystem is capable of making best use of the positive features of the undertaking (Acs et al., 2017).

In itself, the ecosystem is conceptually not suitable for characterizing negative behaviour on the part of the enterprise of a type that is illegal. The territory, as intended in the present study, is not necessarily a virtuous support platform. It is the reality in which the firm is rooted, by means of a series of local relations, reflecting a common vision, a shared history and a specific culture (Golinelli, 2013).

On the basis of this approach, the territorial system is not just a support network. Rather, it has various dimensions by which the firm is influenced and in turn exerts influence, with the undertaking taking positive actions or alternatively taking advantage of its territorial connections to engage in illegal practices.

More needs to be said on this point. It is well known that the attempts to define and delimit the environment in which firms operate, including the geographical and physical space, cannot be limited to the ecosystem, and even less to the territory. Rather, it is necessary to take account of the concept of clusters, while emphasizing the specific dynamics that can be internal to the cluster or function separately, based on the notion of proximity. The two concepts overlap, though separating them out makes it possible not just to identify the distance between them but also the differences between the ecosystem and the territory.

Clusters (Porter, 1998; Delgado et al., 2010) and proximity (Knoben & Oerlemans, 2006; Zimmermann, 2001) are environmental dimensions that in a historical perspective precede the conceptualization of the entrepreneurial ecosystem, while sharing with that concept the following assumptions. Certain driving factors that contribute to the competitive advantage of the firm exist beyond its confines, but within a specific space that for the sake of simplicity may be said to coincide with the administrative confines of the territory (Governa & Salone, 2004).

Institutions, both formal and informal (Casson et al., 2010; North, 1990), and local cultures are usually deemed to be factors favouring cooperation between firms, and instrumental to the normalization of business practices.

Moreover, networks within given areas are conducive to the sharing of knowledge among firms and local actors, such as higher education institutions (Owen-Smith & Powell, 2004), that contribute to a significant extent to the competitive advantage of the firm. In short, the added value for the firm is supported by the resources present in a given geographic rather than being confined to the resources within the firm (Asheim et al., 2011; Porter, 2000).

However, the exact role of firms and how they benefit from these externalities gives rise to the need to distinguish between three concepts. First of all, with regard to clusters, as noted later, the key advantage consists of economies of localization, in which firms benefit from a shared geographic location, thus reducing transport costs and sharing infrastructure costs, or economies of agglomeration, deriving from the opportunity to share the continuous flow of knowledge and the normalization of certain routines and types of know-how (Malmberg & Maskell, 2002). Second, factors of proximity, in particular, geographic proximity, act as drivers, facilitating the exchange of tangible and intangible assets. In third place, entrepreneurial ecosystems are characterized in a similar way by this type of governance of relations and the lack of a well-defined hierarchy or formalized methods of application that hinder the informal interaction between actors (Bell et al., 2009; Pitelis, 2012).

At the same time, there are clear differences from clusters. Ecosystems are not necessarily limited to networks of firms. With regard to networks, in any case, entrepreneurs belonging to a given ecosystem have a greater chance of sharing basic technologies as well as a customer base and market. In many cases due to the fact that ecosystems assign a central role to shared knowledge and technology, they involve various actors, including networks of investors, consultants, mentors and public-sector stakeholders, and thus include higher education institutions, public actors and last but not least the local community. These various stakeholders do not simply provide support for the network, but they themselves become an active part of it. The specific advantage of ecosystems is linked to specific resources that belong to the territory and as a result the space does not act simply as a boundary beyond which the economies of location are no longer effective but it acts as a determinant of the specific features (Audretsch et al., 2019).

In the following the focus will be on the characteristics of clusters and proximities, and on those of ecosystems, and finally the discussion will turn to the notion of territories, highlighting the differences.

1.1.1 Clusters: Characteristics and functions

The most common conceptualization of clusters is provided by Porter (1990). In his view, the key dynamic that identifies clusters is competition, based on the well-known model of the competitive diamond, originally developed to understand the interaction between factors that influence the competitiveness or productivity of firms, industries or countries (Porter, 1990). It is well known that this model originally identified the competitiveness of nations as depending on four factors:

1 *The endowment of factors*: The position of a country in relation to the factors of production, or basic factors (natural resources, climate, geographical location and demographic aspects) and advanced factors (communications, skilled labour, research, technology, education).
2 *The conditions of demand*: For example, strong domestic demand giving rise to sophisticated and demanding customers, which stimulates an improvement in the quality and the manufacture of products that are then highly valued by international consumers, thus maintaining a competitive advantage.
3 *Structure and competition*: The conditions that regulate the way in which firms and internal competition are created, organized and managed, considering the decisive role of internal competition in leading innovation and stimulating the sector.
4 *Correlated and supporting industries*: In the sense of groups (clusters) of industries that facilitate the efficient coordination of production and favour innovation, thus stimulating growth.

As defined by Porter, clusters depend on competition as the driver of development, and this is a dynamic process, as growing firms give rise to increasing demand in correlated sectors and services.

Moreover, according to Porter, competition between firms that are part of a cluster forces firms to innovate. The transition from general to local clusters is the result. The greater the geographical concentration of firms, the more the interaction between the factors constituting the competitive diamond tends to increase.

One aspect of competitive advantage is the location of the firm, considering the narrow confines within which it can manage the interaction with other firms. Cooperation between complementary and specialized firms on the one hand, and the institutions on the other, takes the form of support measures that the territorial government adopts for the development of clusters, such as access to funding, support for knowledge processes and technology transfer. All these factors may interact with each other within a restricted and clearly defined area, where the coordination of a territorial government can promote networking and thus favour cooperation between the actors providing the necessary support. The most significant dimension becomes that of geographic proximity, since a crucial role is recognized for the action of institutions whose scope of intervention is linked to the extension of the territory under management.

As a result, the location of the firm is not important in an absolute sense (in the spatial sense), but rather it is important for firms to be located in close proximity to other firms to favour interaction and collaboration. On the basis of these elements, Porter provides a systematic definition of regional clusters: an informal method of cooperation and interaction between firms belonging to the same sector also involving other firms in the supply chain, government and scientific institutions and other bodies in the same region.

1.1.1.1 Clusters vs. industrial districts

The framing of clusters has been investigated in depth by various authors, and this study examines the conceptual proximity of clusters and Marshall's industrial districts since they are extremely similar notions. As noted earlier, Porter (1990) argues that there is a significant overlap in meaning between the two concepts, indicating a common process: the tendency for businesses to concentrate in geographical terms with a view to gaining certain competitive and operational advantages. To identify the main differences between the concept of clusters and that of industrial districts, highlighting the originality of Porter's theoretical construct, reference may be made to recent studies of clusters, such as the study by the OECD (1996), which integrates Porter's model with the role of institutions engaging in the production of knowledge and technology transfer, that are connected to clusters in the most important phases of the value chain.

In short, the conceptual differences between clusters and industrial districts highlight the fact that districts are clusters of a particular kind, based on geographical proximity concentrated in a limited territory, in which the local community and public interventions in the economy play a substantial role, or at the very least, a role that is more substantial than in clusters. Industrial districts are thus socio-territorial entities characterized by the active presence, in a limited territorial area, determined by natural and historical factors, of a community and a population of industrial firms (Porter & Ketels, 2009). In districts, unlike the case of clusters, communities and firms are interdependent. The fact that the predominant activity is industrial differentiates districts from a generic "economic region". One of the fundamental elements is the concept of "industrial atmosphere": when in a limited geographical area, a significant number of individuals are engaged in the same occupations, trade secrets can no longer be described as such, and a certain level of know-how is developed in an innate manner, "almost by a process of breathing in". In the view of Becattini (1987), one of the leading Italian scholars of industrial districts, that which strongly links firms together in these settings is "a complex and inextricable network of economies and external diseconomies (negative externalities), connections and cost economies, historical and cultural elements, that provide the context for interfirm relations and those that are purely of a personal nature". Business and professional relations are intertwined with social relations of an informal type, thus facilitating the dissemination of knowledge among the actors.

An economic definition that sufficiently encompasses industrial districts must therefore take account not just of the local characteristics listed earlier (territory, community, firms) but also this stable network of interactions and other elements. In more detail, in industrial districts physical proximity counts a great deal, as it facilitates the exchange of information and goods, and the presence of strong socially recognized institutions, giving rise to external economies and favour local firms. On the other hand, a cluster of firms consists of a geographical concentration of companies operating in the same supply chain, more than in the same industrial sector, with strong commercial links with each other. This is often a network of subcontractors working with one or more general contractors and a number of small firms acting as suppliers. Relations between firms in a cluster are usually less complex than between firms in an industrial district, and the physical proximity, although necessary, is less accentuated, to the benefit of long supply chains in a system of global collaboration, also across territories that are geographically distant from each other. The globalization of supply chains can thus be more easily related to the concept of clusters, compared to the traditional concept of industrial districts, historically linked to local "industrial roots".

1.1.1.2 The notion of proximity

Proximity is a key concept in relation to clusters and can be considered in isolation. The idea of examining characteristics and effects separately is useful for understanding whether the benefits that are mainly correlated to elements of vicinity or shared characteristics also apply to spatial dimensions other than clusters and districts, above all in relation to the notion of territory adopted in this study. Basically, while the territory and prior to that the ecosystem is not a cluster, it has in common with the cluster certain elements that are common to clearly defined areas within which economic activities take place.

Proximity is thus a dynamic that needs to be examined because in defining a method of interaction, it carries out, at the same time, a definition of the confines of the area under examination: there is an environmental dimension that terminates where the advantages of proximity reach their limits. A definition of this kind is of greater value than the definition commonly used of an administrative nature, and for the purposes of this study, it plays a more important role. Above all the definition most commonly adopted, and closer to concepts such as areas, confines and vicinity, is the geographic one (Knoben & Oerlemans, 2006).

The reduction of geographic distance gives rise to numerous advantages that are obvious, since every type of material cost relating to transport is reduced. In the same way, physical proximity between individuals improves cooperation, facilitating face-to-face interaction, that is the most efficient way to reduce transaction costs (Bouba-Olga & Ferru, 2012).

The role of geographic factors as part of the process of agglomeration has been analysed by many scholars over a long period of time. Many geo-economic studies concentrate on the advantages of the immediate circulation of information in urbanization processes (Pred, 1966), in particular, the strand of research dealing with the role played by interpersonal contacts in the creation of localized processes of interaction (Utterback, 1974). By way of example, reference may be made to the work of Lucas (1988) examining the reasons why businesses are concentrated in Chicago or Manhattan, although those urban centres are more expensive, and at times inconvenient, although less expensive areas are available everywhere. The reason is simple: businesses want to operate close to each other. Proximity is considered to be a reduction in distance and as a result it is associated with advantages such as visibility, immediacy, and greater clarity about what the business makes available. The concept of geographic proximity rapidly evolved beyond the mere idea of localization/agglomeration, with greater emphasis now placed on a more complex dynamic, aimed at characterizing systems, but also at the structures and organizational processes underlying the systems. It has been shown that localized systems of production are not simply the result of a concentration of firms initially attracted by favourable factors, such as primary resources. Rather, it is the entire development that is constructed on the basis of territorial proximity, including human capital and highly skilled employees (Torre & Portafoglio, 2014).

Geographic proximity is thus a far more complex concept than implied by a simple definition in bidirectional terms. In fact, it consists of horizontal relations that are part of a wider network, characterized by several factors: first, the existence of local institutions that ensure the circulation of local knowledge; second, the specific characteristics of the internal organization of local society; third, the presence of a particular industrial structure based on the existence of ongoing contacts between the local actors. A similar idea is to be found in the analysis of national and local innovation systems (Lundvall, 2007) in which the key role of proximity is demonstrated, in particular thanks to the interactive character of learning processes. The benefits of proximity are transformed into forces of agglomeration, acting on the firms engaged in processes of interaction.

Proximity is not the sole geographic element that is based on the concept of distance. In addition to transport costs and the scarcity of land, other factors act as a vehicle for the processes of localization. Marshall (1890) was the first to bring together the concept of externalities, local atmosphere and industrial secrets, paving the way for a research strand that over the years has extended the concept of proximity to include characteristics other than spatial-geographical features.

Social proximity implies the sharing (and acceptance) of formal provisions (laws, property rights) and informal rules (unwritten rules) that take the form of traditions, taboos and codes of conduct (Agrawal et al., 2008). More specifically, this type of proximity consists of working conditions, regulations and accounting systems, but it is also a matter of routines and shared cultural expectations, based on history, custom and traditions (Zeller, 2004). In both senses, social proximity seems to favour collective learning through "a common space of representation" (Capello, 1999), referring to actors who belong to the same network of relations. On the one hand, it is possible to identify a sense of belonging to the same community of practice and thus a position occupied in the network of relations; on the other hand, a level of – social – similarity is perceptible between the organizations in the network. Social proximity can thus be intended respectively in terms of structural equivalence and of embeddedness (Andersen, 2013). Its advantages consist of the capacity to facilitate the exchange of tacit knowledge, and to encourage behaviour based on "communicative rationale" rather than simply on an "economic rationale", thus, improving the mutual learning process, development and innovation (Bertoncin et al., 2015).

It has been pointed out that organizations that are similar from a cultural point of view collaborate more easily and more efficiently, since the sharing of systems of interpretation and routines enables organizations to reduce the risks of misunderstanding and the costs of knowledge transfer (Knoben & Oerlemans, 2006). Moreover, the specific advantages of cultural proximity have been examined in certain economic sectors. In the banking industry, Fisman et al. (2017) have shown that the sharing of norms and ethical codes, religious beliefs and ethnic traditions improves the allocation of loans, mitigating problems of asymmetrical information. In the pharmaceutical industry, Zeller (2004) has argued that cultural proximity facilitates the flow of information within the firm, and between the firm and other organizations.

Finally, technological proximity can be understood as the "tools, devices and knowledge that mediate between inputs and outputs (process technology) and/or that create new products or services (product technology). Technological proximity refers not to these technologies themselves, but to the knowledge actors possess about these technologies" (Knoben & Oerlemans, 2006). A number of scholars (Harhoff, 2000; Autant-Bernard, 2001) have analysed the role of technological proximity in fostering innovation, and the role of knowledge spillovers. Orlando (2004) has noted that spillovers are most frequent between technologies in proximity with each other, and as a result the ability to make knowledge productive in another firm depends on the overall degree of technological proximity. The points of contact with the cognitive dimension of proximity are evident. As argued by Meeus and Oerlemans (2005), different forms of proximity tend to be interrelated in intricate ways. The problem of the relationship between various kinds of proximity is significant both in conceptual and applicational terms. Various studies (Knoben & Oerlemans, 2006; Bertoncin et al., 2015) examine the interconnections between different kinds of proximity and in particular the relation between geographic and organizational proximity, and between geographic and cognitive proximity. In spite of these efforts, it is still problematic to carry out an empirical assessment of the relations of causality and the interconnections between proximities (Bertoncin et al., 2015).

1.1.2 Ecosystems of firms

Our attention now turns to ecosystems of firms, which constitutes a more recent conceptualization compared to clusters (Spigel & Harrison, 2018). As noted earlier, since this concept is based on the binomial distinction between firms and the territory, it shares certain characteristics with clusters, though in some respects it is different. The innovative aspect of the concept of ecosystems is that it highlights the variety of roles of the actors, while attenuating certain aspects of clusters, such as the specificity of a merceological sector, and assigning greater importance to technological and socio-cultural aspects.

Ecosystems are thus not necessarily limited to networks of firms. When reference is made to these systems, in any case, entrepreneurs who are part of the ecosystem are more likely to deploy the same technological resources rather than having a common customer base or market. But often, due to the fact that assigns a central role to shared knowledge or technology, the ecosystem involves a range of actors, including a network of investors, consultants and mentors, while being open to stakeholders not necessarily in the private sector, thus including higher education institutions, public bodies and the local communities. These other actors do not simply play a supporting role, but become an active part of the network. The particular advantages of an ecosystem are linked to specific resources belonging to the territory, and as a result the area does not simply serve to delimit the boundaries of the system beyond which the economies of localization no longer apply (Manimala & Wasdani, 2015) but it is the factor that determines the specific nature of the actors and the resources involved. The set of actors involved is more extensive. The complexity of the system, that is one of its natural characteristics, also depends on the heterogeneous character of the actors involved. In clusters, actors other than firms are often confined to a support role, whereas in ecosystems they perform a different function, as active subjects, and they form part of a network facilitating the circulation of knowledge that enhances the contribution of all the actors involved.

The network consists not just of entrepreneurs but also of investors, mentors, highly skilled employees, university research centres and local customers. The interactions that characterize these ecosystems are marked by their proximity, and are predominantly social and technological, and only territorial at a secondary level (Meshram & Rawani, 2019).

As a result, the network consists of a range subjects who are in "technological proximity" coming together to create a knowledge-based network, sharing their skills and improving their competences and enhancing their knowledge by disseminating information. The network is reinforced by social proximity, including the sharing of an entrepreneurial culture that favours risk-taking linked to business activities that can exploit this knowledge transmission. Since the actors taking part are also from the public sector, there is an administrative and geographical limit beyond which these actors may not exercise their powers. In essence, in ecosystems geographic proximity does not overlap with administrative confines, unlike the geographic proximity of clusters that is characterized by economies of agglomeration closely linked to the skills available within the firm (Owen-Smith & Powell, 2004).

In the following a more detailed account is given of the three types of proximity and the benefits they confer on firms, as well as on the system considered as a whole. First of all, technological proximity brings firms together for the purposes of sharing knowledge and skills. Technological proximity functions as a means of selection of the actors taking part in the ecosystem, since it represents the channel by which market-based technological information is gathered and circulated, enabling firms to gain access to funding, influencing business prospects and the acquisition of skills (Shane & Cable, 2002). Investment capital is self-evidently the means by which investors contribute to the system, since the choices made reflect their technological preferences and at a practical level have an impact on business decision-making, in particular with regard to new business ventures. The presence of local investors with close links to the business community is thus a significant catalyst for the growth of firms (Jackson, 2011). In addition, dealmakers have a role to play within systems characterized by technological proximity. These are actors with a high level of social capital who proactively promote new connections contributing to an improvement in training and business growth within ecosystems. They live and operate in a particular region and take responsibility for the management of local operations (Feldman & Zoller, 2016). Finally, mention should be made of the employees, who are characterized by technological proximity based on skills. High levels of human capital are the key to success in the knowledge economy, and high levels of specialization on the part of the workforce are a key component of company competitiveness, in particular innovative skills (Barnes-Mauthe et al., 2015). A further key element for the success of ecosystems is the cultural alignment of the skilled workforce with the company. An employee who is inclined to take risks is clearly a further advantage of proximity, in connection with the cultural proximity characterizing the ecosystem (Brondizio et al., 2009). Social proximity brings together the actors in an ecosystem by sharing the culture of the enterprise along with its history.

A number of scholars have examined how local cultural perspectives influence the wider process of regional entrepreneurship (Brown & Mason, 2017). Certain rules, certain practices, but in a more general sense certain values underlying the entrepreneurial process are the outcome of a local learning process, and are handed down and shared within a given geographical space. Many studies have highlighted local differences according to various processes of social proximity: cultural attitudes and, as a result of these attitudes, a different way of taking on business risks give rise to radical differences between entrepreneurship in different geographic areas. Environments with a business culture with a high propensity to take risks tend to normalize highly risky choices as those that need to be made regardless of the fact that other choices are possible (Kibler et al., 2014).

Systems in which the local culture is inspired by entrepreneurial success stories disseminated by political campaigns as models to be emulated encourage local start-ups to follow similar routes (Malecki, 2018a). Examples of successful entrepreneurs within a particular community are often considered case studies or testimonials in universities or high schools within the region. Students learn and internalize a successful entrepreneurial model that helps to ensure a number of emerging entrepreneurs within the region, inspired by a business culture they have been exposed to during their formative years (Stam & Spigel, 2016).

Moreover, certain elements of ecosystems are characterized by geographical proximity, as they have a tangible presence in the region. For example, universities create networks as they are located in a physical space in the same geographic region as the firms with which they form an ecosystem. The main resource provided by universities consists of the development of new technologies that have an impact on and are in turn affected by the technologies adopted by enterprises (Prokop, 2021).

Companies are capable of accessing the knowledge produced by universities by hiring graduates or commissioning research, or by means of informal exchanges in the form of spillovers, such as presentations by university lecturers or workshops open to the public. Universities help to develop the human capital in a given region, at the same time promoting an entrepreneurial mentality among students, while encouraging them to set up new enterprises (Marotta, 2007). In addition, public actors promote policies of value for the region where they are located.

Funding schemes, tax incentives and the investment of public funds are a fundamental part of the economic and political setting in which entrepreneurs operate. This context can result in the removal of legal barriers to the setting up of companies, effective tax regimes, or the provision of public funds to support entrepreneurship, creating networks or incubation programmes. Although the effectiveness of policies promoting entrepreneurship is debatable (Ombi et al., 2018), the political context is still an important factor for defining the confines of regional entrepreneurship.

Finally, the effect of local markets with strong demand is a fundamental element in terms of opportunities within entrepreneurial ecosystems. The presence of a local customer base gives rise to opportunities for new firms and encourages entrepreneurial spin-offs (Spilling, 1996; Bedő et al., 2020). Entrepreneurs are in a privileged position to identify opportunities in local markets due to the fact that interaction is facilitated by geographic proximity.

1.1.3 The territory: Specific concept, autonomous notion?

The aforementioned discussion clearly shows how the spatial environment has acquired an increasing value that is more sophisticated than in the early stages of studies in this field. The concept of proximity provides an important contribution to understanding the fundamental traits of the evolution of the geographical location of firms. From clusters to ecosystems, the key features of proximity undergo certain changes, carrying a different weight and above all becoming more complex.

In its original version, the cluster does not reveal much about the territory, except merely as an area in which firms are located, consisting of the geographical proximity that is the preferential criterion of the configuration. With the concept of industrial districts delineated by Marshall, the idea of industrial atmosphere was widened to include proximity that is social as well as geographical as a further advantage of clusters. In ecosystems, the spatial confines delimiting a place within which to benefit from geographical proximity are less clearly defined, because technological and social proximity involving the various actors in the network play a more central role in terms of the economies of scale and scope made available by the system. Geographical proximity, as noted above, overlaps with the territorial spaces of the region within which the public authorities promote policies supporting business.

On closer inspection, social proximity is closely connected to the relational dynamics of Marshall's industrial districts. The network is characterized by a set of attitudes, cultural norms and entrepreneurial beliefs that can be projected onto the territory by other actors within the region. This gives rise to an entrepreneurial territorial culture that develops in a network that is then transmitted to the territory, but it does not consist of the territorial culture strictly speaking. Essentially, although ecosystems bring in innovative elements compared to clusters, and give more importance to the role of territories, they are still closely connected to the logic of clusters. A particular territorial area is taken into consideration because it coincides with a network of actors, due to their physical presence but it is not an autonomous unit: the values of the territory are those of the firms located in that territory. The relations with the territory are network relations, mainly of a technological kind. However, this conceptualization fails to take account of a series of processes that are also important to understand the relations between the firm and the territory. A direct relationship between a particular company and the territory, extrapolated from a network of agents, does not find a conceptualization within the ecosystem. Let us imagine a firm that transfers the culture of the enterprise as a model of behaviour for the local population, without any need for further communicative processes. Then imagine the opposite situation in which it is the territory that has an impact on the firm or on an entire network of firms. What is missing is the ability to understand certain relations that are however important, and that go beyond the idea of a complex system constructed by numerous agents connected with one another. Also missing is the potential of application of the ecosystem to the negative aspects of company behaviour. Certain kinds of behaviour by firms that are illegal might also be territorial, but it is difficult to claim that they are part of systemic perspectives that are functional, giving rise to benefits of proximity that are by definition perfectly legal, and even more difficult to imagine them being associated with illicit behaviour. The territory is essentially part of the network, and not something surrounding the network. The idea of the territory that this study is based on is derived from studies in the field of economic geography (Dicken & Malmberg, 2001) and it has an application in management studies that is of growing importance (Simone et al., 2018).

The focal point of this conceptualization is that territories should be considered an autonomous unit of analysis in relation to firms. Territories consist of a series of economic and socio-cultural relations, including those with firms or an individual firm. This is a vision that places territories at the centre of the discussion and reconfigures the logical order of things. Territories can be repositioned as intelligent containers, or rather as accumulators of resources (Malmberg et al., 1996), in particular of knowledge, that provides a rich substratum of specific resources (Capello, 2009). Territories precede and do not exist because they are exclusively legitimated by networks, as they are the outcome of all the co-creations over time by means of the interaction between nature and human behaviour, the way resources are exploited, the way they manage tensions and conflicts, and the mode of coexistence. Territories are therefore a mechanism (Foucault, 2007), an explosive force (Lussault, 2007) and a product of human activity and of the culture of the human population that settles in a given territory (Painter, 2010). Territories consist not just of organizations but also of individuals and they develop thanks to complex relations taking place among the multiplicity of actors and the diversity of relations within their confines (Lundquist et al., 2014).

By concentrating on the links between these elements and the territory, it is possible to interpret the territory as a network, as a connective tissue and relational space, that depends exclusively on the actions of the community living there (Simone et al., 2017). These actions consist of a variety of processes (natural, social, technical and economic) carried out by a wide range of actors. At the same time, each process contains the territory and, in turn, each process is contained in the territory. Essentially, unlike ecosystems, and even before that, clusters, the relationship is bidirectional, it can be identified with a number of actors, and it does not necessarily lead to virtuous outcomes.

In addition, every territory is unique, since it is characterized by its own relational capital both territorial and cultural (Zamagni, 2008), as well as its history that often coincides with the history of the firms operating there, and with the local customs that have an impact on local networks and local identity. These considerations lead to a characterization of the territory as a spatially defined society of which entrepreneurial ecosystems or clusters of firms represent a specific instance while not fully sharing its confines. For conceptual reasons, the dynamics of the entrepreneurial ecosystem are reflected in the territory, with the participation of a range of actors, and the nature of the territory is defined not so much by the firms but rather by a more complex idea of society.

Finally, there is a need to clarify how proximity characterizes the extension of the territory. The territory embodies in equal measure all three types of proximity, without necessarily giving greater importance to any of them. Mainly due to the fact that it is a wider network of relations less clearly defined than those of a cluster, the territory consists of geographic, social and technological proximity, the characteristics of which, unlike clusters and ecosystems, are unique, to the point that no territory is able to replicate the characteristics of another. Table 1.1 provides an overview of these concepts.

Table 1.1 Main characteristics of the environment

Environmental dimensions	*Key actors*	*Main kind of proximity*	*Role of the territory*	*Nature of relations*
Clusters	Firms in the supply chain	Geographic	Territorial area	Within the cluster
Districts	Firms in the same sector	Geographic Social	Territorial area	Within the district determined by the environment
Entrepreneurial ecosystems	Firms and other actors in networks	Technological	Functional units of analysis	Within the network determined by the environment
Territories	Societies consisting of a range of actors	Geographic Social Technological	Separate units of analysis	Within the network or considered one by one, either licit or illicit

1.2 The organizational dimension: Structural design, power configurations and organizational culture

This chapter deals with the micro-organizational aspects of the analysis, examined as organizational tools that traditionally operate by linking the firms with their environment. This chapter then examines the strong territorial characterization of the combination of key concepts that constitute power, the organizational configuration and various organizational cultures. The analysis is carried out by means of three case studies in which the firm interacts with the surrounding territory, through its organizational dimension.

1.2.1 Introductory remarks

From the overview above, it is clear that firms inevitably cultivate relations with the surrounding territory, and that the firm and the territory are closely connected, as actors constituting the same system. Firms are set up and develop in a physical and human environment that conditions them, and that in turn is conditioned by the organization of production that takes shape and evolves. As a result, an intersection of relations and values is put in place. Moreover, on the basis of the characterization of the territory outlined above, the relationship between the firm and the territory is not influenced by the size and nature of the firm. This means that small and medium-sized enterprises, and also large firms, can be characterized by the complex territorial collocation which, as noted above, constitutes a cultural and social construction capable of determining elements of identity, networks of relations and social cohesion. However, what matters is the means by which this interaction takes place, taking advantage of the organizational dimensions of the firm, rather than the characteristics that distinguish it from other firms. From this point of view, the relationship with the territory can be compared to the relationship between the firm and the environment as traditionally framed in organization theory (Weick, 1969; Thompson, 1967).

The interaction between the firm and the environment, like the interaction between the firm and the territory, takes place by means of dynamic processes, *mutatis mutandis* characterized by common elements. As a result, two arguments may be put forward. The first is that the firm is not an isolated entity, and would have no chance of surviving without constant interaction with the actors beyond its confines. The second is that interaction exploits the organizational dimension of the firm. In other words, it benefits from organizational elements that allow it to operate beyond the confines of the enterprise, promoting a continuous dialectic with that which goes beyond the limits of the firm. This means that an attempt will be made to provide a theoretical overview of the relations between the firm and the territory, with a view to comparing the salient characteristics, comparing the traditional exchange relations between the firm and the environment with the relations between the firm and the territorial system.

1.2.2 *Insights into open systems and the environment in which firms operate*

The characterization of the firm as a unit of analysis over and above the idea of a closed box, but rather considered as a constant system of interaction with the environment, is an assumption adopted not only in organization theory but also in a number of disciplines that take the firm as the focus of investigation (March, 1962; Lesourne, 1976; Dierkes & Preston, 1977).

Without claiming to provide an exhaustive account, and focusing on organizational studies, it is possible to take the concept of open systems as the theoretical starting point to consider the nature of the relationship between the firm and the territory as the key to the interpretation of the existence of the firm, and thus to delineate the confines of the firm in a more flexible manner than in previous studies (Kast & Rosenzweig, 1972). Firms are considered to be open systems as they are characterized by interdependent activities aimed at constructing "unstable coalitions" for the participants, while being rooted in the environment, and dependent on continuous exchanges with that environment (Scott & Davis, 2015).

In this perspective, the environment becomes crucial to the life of any organization as the firm exists by means of interaction, constantly acquiring tangible and intangible assets, and in turn acting as a provider of such assets. The next step in theoretical terms is based on an understanding of the characteristics of the environment: firms with a greater capacity for survival are those that strengthen their organizational dimensions not only on the basis of their own objectives but also in a way that is functional to the environment on which they depend. Moreover, environmental characteristics tend to determine the structural and behavioural configurations that are most suitable for the development of the relationship between the organization and the environment in an optimal manner, which according to the point of view adopted, can be long-lasting, efficient and virtuous (Staber & Sydow, 2002).

Constructing an argument based on key concepts and with a certain amount of simplification, it is possible to map an environment in close proximity to the firm, and an environment that is not in such close proximity. Reference may be made to a model of concentric circles: the outer circle represents a general environment that includes any actor or process external to the firm, with a capacity to influence its decisions, whereas the inner circle more specifically represents those dynamics and actors that exert a direct impact on the firm while also being subject to the influence of the firm. In generic terms, the specific environment has a typical subject that makes it possible to identify its confines and characteristics. This generally means stakeholders, those actors whose interests are fundamental for the choices of the organization and vice versa, whereas the more general environment consists of actors who are not directly in the range of action of the firm, meaning they have a capacity to exert an influence, and to be influenced, that is less immediate than in the case of stakeholders.

1.2.3 The environment, characteristics and organizational configuration: Power relations

The relationship with the environment is characterized mainly by the three organizational dimensions of the firm: power relations, organizational configurations and culture.[1]

An examination of power relations as a means of interaction starts from the observation that the success of the firm depends on exchanges. More specifically, the survival of the firm depends on a certain number of exchanges with external actors. Exchanges are characterized by a greater or lesser degree of power according to the level of dependency of the parties to the exchange. According to Thompson (1967), an organization depends on a number of providers in its specific environment in proportion to its need for the resources (tangible and intangible) that each element can provide, in an inverse relation on the basis of the alternative providers supplying the same resources. It is rarely the case that the exchange is based on equal power between the parties and an equivalent level of dependency (Emerson, 2019). However, the task of the organization is to maximize its power, that is, to create links of dependency that are active, and to reduce its own level of dependency. In this sense, a firm should be constantly engaged in seeking alternative sources for the purposes of enhancing its autonomy and reducing its dependency. In order to maximize its power by increasing the dependence of the external environment, the firm can expand its resources, whereas to reduce its dependency, the exchange mechanism needs to be based on networks (Hill & Chen, 2006).

Essentially, each node within the network provides opportunities for transactions, with at least one other actor within a given set: the network, thus, consists of a structure with mutual opportunities, the characteristics of which will vary based on the type of exchanges, the frequency and the nature of the exchange. Each element within the network constitutes a different configuration, not only in terms of the allocation of resources but also in terms of the power relations inherent in the element. Firms generally operate across a number of networks, occupying different positions of power. Finally, from a merely quantitative point of view, the number of networks in which the firm does business increases the complexity of the environment in which it operates (Malecki, 2018b).

To sum up, the characteristics of the environment are the outcome of the relations that the firm establishes within its environment. As such they depend on but do not precede the organization. Power is a key variable. It is a synonym of autonomy, and its absence gives rise to dependence on other actors operating within the same environment.

1.2.3.1 Organizational configuration and the environment

There is another form of interaction with the environment that is not so closely linked to exchange relations and that is more closely related to the limits imposed by natural factors in the interaction between the firm and the environment. In this case, the interaction depends on the capacity to carry out structural adaptations to the environmental characteristics: firms undergo changes, taking on new configurations, and such reconfigurations enable them to respond in a timely manner to environmental changes. The degree of environmental variability may be seen as a function of three main characteristics: first, the frequency of changes in the pertinent environmental activities; second, the degree of difference between the various changes; third, the degree of irregularity in the global model of change. However, there appears to be a general consensus: the greater the environmental variability and the uncertainty deriving from it, the greater the need for the organizational structure of the firm to adapt, and to be continually redefined (Burns & Stalker, 1961; Hage & Aiken, 1967; Lawrence & Lorsch, 1967).

This redefinition concerns interventions relating to organizational planning, including the strengthening and/or specialization of operational units, as well as access to information and more general dynamics of coordination. The principle remains the same: environmental inputs give rise to a variety of restrictions that are so severe as to lead to a transformation of the identity of the organization where this is necessary for survival. Structural adaptation can take place in two ways, the first of which gives greater importance to the individual operational units. The qualitative and quantitative changes concerning these units reflect the uncertainty and the complexity of the related sub-environments, considered on the basis of their proximity to these units (Lawrence & Lorsch, 1967). The second places greater emphasis on the organic or mechanical model of the responses of each unit to the environment, dealing with bureaucratic constraints, centralized decision-making and formalized roles with more fluid, less management models capable of supporting less formal roles and decentralized decision-making (Burns & Stalker, 1961; Wilkesmann & Wilkesmann, 2018). The distance between the two models depends on the instability of the environment that operates along a continuum the extremities of which are represented by the two paradigm models.

1.2.3.2 The environment and the culture of the firm

The corporate culture must necessarily be consistent with the environmental culture from which it derives (Allaire & Firsirotu, 1984; Gordon, 1991). Suffice it to refer to the value of gender issues in the workplace, considered to be central in most Western countries, but totally absent in those countries in which there is a primary workforce that is male, and another, secondary and complementary, that is female. It is not even necessary to imagine that such a conception is intrinsic to societies that are distant in terms of evolution and in geographic terms. In an environmental perspective, culture has an impact on the corporate culture above all with regard to employment and the working environment, expectations and the related beliefs, that are the "raw material" of corporate culture.

The environmental culture is often linked to the institutional culture of a given society (Lysova et al., 2019), above all to the rules that the country adopts to establish rights, duties and in general all the matters relating to the employment relationship. There is also a more specific level of the culture in a given sector, relating to values, beliefs and the rules applied that differentiate one sector from another. It has been argued that this subdivision, though rarely examined in depth, is essential because it represents the way of doing business in a given sector, and is closely linked to the survival of the firm (Zhao et al., 2018). Both the social culture, and that of the specific sector in which a firm operates, constitute a context that is important for understanding corporate culture. Arguably corporate culture is shaped by relations with industrial culture and social norms, and by means of this relation, it becomes an institutional system of internal management that is both legitimate and recognized (Kwarteng & Aveh, 2018). Finally, what counts is the compatibility with the environmental culture, conditioned by a series of internal conditions that may be summarized as follows: first, the cultural and institutional pressure exerted by large firms in relation to smaller ones in the same sector, not always in compliance with and at times in violation of the institutional framework; second, the life cycle of the firm, giving rise to the need for a different corporate culture;

third, strategies for growth, often the most evident expression of the values guiding the firm; fourth, monitoring systems, as the corporate culture depends in part on the systems the organization has set up for monitoring its activities, including the formal structure, financial management systems and human resource strategies (Pathiranage et al., 2020).

1.2.4 *The characterization of the territory as a specific environment*

Bringing together the organizational literature relating to the environment and the organizational dimensions and the conceptualization of the territorial system in the discussion above, it is possible to cast light on how the firm can use its organizational dimensions to interact with the territory, that is conceived as a system of socio-economic relations. The means by which the firm exerts an influence and is itself influenced is related to the organizational dimensions as characterized by the territory, emphasizing the fact that the characterization of the territory is of a dual nature, as it can represent the means by which the firm is rooted in the territory, but also the impact on that firm on the part of the territory, of a hybrid nature, both social and economic, reflected in the organizational dimension.

1.2.4.1 *Territorial power (exerting influence and being influenced)*

As noted above, in the relation between the firm and the territory, power acts as a mechanism for the distribution and allocation of resources, with the firm in a position of dependency or autonomy. The exercise of power at territorial level in both directions can have positive and negative implications, in any case of a different kind compared to the exercise of power in a general and specific environment. Taking a positive view, exchanges imply the use of resources of a highly specific territorial kind, meaning that resources are relatively scarse but research costs are reduced. This exercise of power takes place on the basis of a relationship of trust that is easier to achieve thanks to the interpersonal relations within the territory that tend to be more stable (Sridharan & Simatupang, 2013), and due to the expectation that local trading practices will be complied with, along with the customs in a particular territory, and to the increased possibility of knowledge and monitoring on the part of those involved in exchanges in a clearly defined geographic area. The territory tends to mitigate asymmetrical power relations: as a result, it is less likely for a territorial exchange to give rise to a totally inequitable distribution of resources. In this way, power relations are not eliminated but rather channelled into ongoing interactions that are beneficial to the territory in relational terms. In this type of exchange, as noted above, the characteristics of the market and of society as a whole facilitate the exercise of power in accordance with mechanisms of gradually increasing levels of trust (Dyer & Singh, 1998). Both are needed, and it is also the case that if those aspects of the transaction not determined by commercial considerations are missing, the remaining part of the transaction is reduced to an exchange of territorial resources but the territorial characterization of power is missing. In this perspective, this relationship produces negative effects that are far superior to the effects of an exchange relationship with no territorial dimension. Essentially, unless accompanied by a common socio-cultural denominator, the benefits arising from the use of local resources, such as highly skilled labour or raw materials sourced locally, constitute a specific investment not mitigated by economic benefits deriving from social relations (Grandori, 1997), with costs that are significantly higher than in a non-territorial exchange. The firm may exert territorial power or depend on territorial resources ensuring stability and efficiency in exchanges that are greater than in non-territorial exchanges, but at the same time may take unfair advantage of a position of power favoured by certain territorial elements while not respecting certain other elements, with negative implications that are greater than those in a non-territorial exchange. There are many virtuous examples of firms that set up the entire supply chain within their own territory, with levels of technological innovation and creativity that would be inconceivable without a cultural approach that recognizes the territorial value of relations with the territories in which production and sales are located. It is a matter of striking a complex balance, in which there is a risk of rent-seeking arising from the existence of a specific relationship with the territory (Valdaliso & Wilson, 2015).

1.2.4.2 Organizational configuration and the environment

Reference was made above to environmental processes and their capacity to condition organizational structures (Yasai-Ardekani, 1989): these structures change according to the variability of the environment, constituting one of the most significant responses by the organization to environmental inputs. However, the transfer of this assumption from the general concept of the environment to the more specific notion of the territory gives rise to the need for further explanation. Rather than reasoning in terms of the degree of environmental variability, it makes sense to reason in terms of the degree of variability of territories. It is the unique properties of a given territory compared to other territories that has an impact on the organizational configuration.

Framing the dynamics of organizational configuration in territorial terms means ensuring that a firm presents structural configurations that change according to inputs from the territory, involving the entire model or individual functional units, to the point of focusing on individual elements of micro-organizational planning. With regard to the first aspect, that is, the choice of model with mechanical or organic characteristics, the interventions may concern four distinct factors: the number of levels in the hierarchy, the range of actions taken for supervisory purposes, the reduction of staffing levels, and the inversion between direct and indirect employment (El Talla et al., 2018). Reconfiguring the overall structure may result in the need for a close combination of these factors, for example, through the reduction in the number of levels in the hierarchy, while extending the range of actions for supervisory purposes, and at the same time rethinking staffing levels to reduce the overall number, and the relative resources allocated, while transferring line management from direct employment to a series of functions hitherto carried out by specialized staff units (human resources, procurement of technical and productive resources). This is an intervention aimed at flattening the organizational structure that may be carried out with regard to the entire structure and the context (Rezaee et al., 2018). The most innovative experiences in this field are to be found in companies in the service sector, or in those firms where the service component is increasingly important within the system of production. In these contexts, firms that are most innovative in terms of their relations and systems for providing services within the territory do so because the territory recognizes and appreciates the level of services offered above all based on experience and the added value deriving from the exchange (Carayannis et al., 2022). This is considered part of a long lasting and stable relationship, less and less dominated by a logic of economic transaction, and increasingly characterized by a logic of partnership in the joint production of services, with mutual learning processes.

Many banking services, particularly in the case of banks with a strong territorial identity (section 5), present these characteristics. In particularly significant cases, the joint production of services to respond to territorial demands is considered to be a factor fostering territorial development. In the same way, a firm may envisage interventions leading to an organizational reconfiguration concerning particular functions, as they provide a close connection with the territory. At macro level, Hofstede (1980) has demonstrated how the culture of country can influence the choices made by firm across the board, ranging from strategies to business models resulting in changes in the organizational configuration. Multinationals set up operations in various countries taking account of the fact that they are based in the home country and that certain choices made at the peripheral level are not necessarily replicated in other businesses in other countries at a decentralized level. The various territories provide input in terms of human resources management, procurement procedures, business practices, models and procedures for the local management of resources, leading to the identification of appropriate solutions, not allowing for any exceptions. The firm internalizes the elements that are important for the territory both in terms of recognition and a sense of belonging (Del Baldo, 2012).

Essentially, there are two inputs that the territory can provide to cast light on interventions for organizational reconfiguration. The territory is characterized by a series of constraints while at the same time providing business opportunities for the firm. The firm makes a number of design choices against a cultural and administrative background of standard practices that have been put into place during the historical development of the territory. The firm may well find itself in a position of path dependency in relation to the territory: the organizational configuration is likely to depend on the nature of external networks with which it is involved at territorial level (Hassink, 2005). In other words, there is a more extensive network that is established at territorial level, the configuration of which is reflected in the organizational configuration of the firm. Key structural elements such as the corporate hierarchy, control mechanisms, ownership structures and traditional contractual arrangements tend to be mitigated within more complex networks that give rise to structural changes, at least in relation to the operational units directly involved in the networks (Kleiner & Karpinskaya, 2019). In many countries, non-profit bodies are involved in joint production schemes, the contents of which are rooted in the local territory. In providing services in the social sector, non-profit bodies often operate as part of networks together with public bodies and members of the public who benefit from their services, jointly planning, managing and delivering social services of various kinds. The nature of this joint production has immediate implications for the functional units directly involved in the collective processes, with the result that the organizational architecture is modified on the basis of the needs of the territory. The nature of the change is without doubt territorial and reflects the degree of importance and the types of collective intervention that a territory considers to be crucial in terms of personal services.

1.2.4.3 Interactions between organizational and territorial culture

One of the most important dimensions of the territory discussed above concerns the wealth of intangible assets that in all probability constitute the most significant resource for the territory. There is a fine line between the culture and history of a territory as these processes are shaped in parallel over time, and thus move forward together. The culture of a territory depends on the capacity of the local population to transform the fundamental resources of the territory over time, with the result that they become increasingly complex, capable of entering into closely connected market networks (Labianca et al., 2020). Historical developments mean that territorial factors including geographic, environmental, ecological, social, political, cultural and economic features are subject to change, along with employment as a factor of transformation.

As noted above, territorial culture constitutes a major restraint for corporate culture, but the reverse is also the case. A firm can have the capacity to intervene and influence local culture. In both instances, firms are characterized by the fact that they are rooted in the local territory (Baù et al., 2019). In any case, the firm considers its connections with the local territory as a fundamental resource. The territory is deemed to be an enormous repository of resources and knowledge, and a fertile ground for business: the firm was set up in this particular territory, it carries on its operations there and it is distinguished by its specific features. The territory is considered to be a shared resource, since it constitutes the essential environment for the material reproduction of human life and the realization of socio-cultural relations and public life (Simone et al., 2018). In this sense, the constitutive dimension of the corporate culture consists of the recognition of the value of the territory. More specifically, numerous studies have shown that in different ways the local culture has the ability to influence the culture of the firm, both in positive and negative terms (Kashner, 1990; Ucar, 2018). Territories endowed with high levels of social capital are those in which it is unusual for firms to be involved in cases of fraud or corruption, or in a manner that has even more impact on the local community, in illegal practices causing environmental damage (Miller & Le Breton-Miller, 2021). A number of studies adopt the concept of environmental embeddedness to explain how a culture of security of the territory is reflected in a culture of security of the firms operating in that territory (Dekker & Hasso, 2016; Sharafizad et al., 2022). However, many other instances can be found relating to the choice of values and local customs, often capable of having an impact on the know-how of the firm. In wine producing firms, for example, the production processes are the outcome of a learning process based on local traditions, with centuries-old occupations that survive even today as a specific component of the know-how, constituting a close bond between the firms and the traditions that have been internalized within the firm as elements of originality that are carried over into the markets, but as argued above, the opposite may also be the case.

The Italian case of Olivetti (now part of TIM) is often cited as a case in which the local roots mean that a virtuous business model can become a cultural model. As argued by Simone et al. (2019), this is an example of a

> company that absorbed the local culture then created local culture, resulting in an evident improvement in terms of the territorial system that probably cannot be replicated outside its natural habitat. This company is closely linked to all the stakeholders and all the systems that make up its territory, creating a complex and synergic network consisting of local production and social and cultural rights. It is a responsible firm in which, in addition to production, attention is paid to the reproduction of resources – human, tangible and intangible – as well as the traditions and culture of the territory (our translation)

utilized during the process of production.

It is not just how the firm builds up a network, ensuring stability over time and consolidating a network of relations based on trust (Crouch et al., 2001;

Table 1.2 Systemic vs. territorial organizational dimensions

	Organizational dimension and system	*Organizational dimension and territory*
Power	Generic resource exchange with environmental actors.	Resource exchange of a highly specific territorial kind.
Organizational configuration	Structural adaptation to the environment.	Structural adaptation to the territory.
Culture	National and international formal norms; sectorial formal and informal norms.	Territorial formal and informal norms.

Ostrom, 2009). It is also a matter of promoting inclusive policies, actions and local sustainability, maintaining a virtuous ongoing relationship with the employees with the result that Olivetti is identified as a territorial firm promoting territorial development. The natural habitat of Olivetti is well known for its high level of human capital. It may even be said that a positive domino effect ensures that the employment relations as conceived by Olivetti are relations that provide incentives and advanced training opportunities at local level. There is, however, a particular culture of production that is pervasive at all social levels and in all employment grades in the area, and the firm is influenced by this high level of social capital. Finally, it is most likely that the corporate culture and the local culture are intertwined in a virtuous cycle, with the result that it is hard to trace the dividing line between one and the other, and to determine which prevails over the other. In many cases one and the other are indistinguishable and above all capable of co-existing and reinforcing each other.

Finally, Table 1.2 compares organizational dimensions based on the systemic approach to organizational dimensions based on the territorial approach.

1.2.5 Case study

1.2.5.1 Case study no. 1: Business and territory: Filipino street food

The stories of entrepreneurs are often tales of resilience, passion and talent. There are stories however of everyday heroes with an important connection to the territory. These stories often relate how a challenge was overcome with the territory as an ally. An in-depth knowledge of the territory means having an understanding of its potential, because if it is properly exploited, that potential can be capitalized on not just for the individual entrepreneur but for the community as a whole that is present in that territory. The story of Florencio Escabas is that of a restaurant owner in Cordova, a small village in the Philippines. This story is based on an eel soup together with the dream of increasing the prosperity of the community thanks to a combination of his own experience and the local traditions. His story is that of a fisherman who sought to feed his family over a period of 30 years. Eels are said to be easy to fish and to be rich in fat, and thus have a considerable capacity to sate the appetite: rich food at a low cost. The first part of the story of Florencio before he became an entrepreneur is thus characterized by a logic of efficiency. The transition from fishing to low-cost catering is a relatively short step. Florencio cooked eels, attempting to make a dish with a flavour that was not too strong, using the recipes from his community to cook a variety of fish. Florencio Escabas created the *nilarang*, the favourite dish in Cordova.

His small stand quickly turned into large-scale event known as the *nilarang* of Cordova, a tourist attraction that became world famous, with reports in the press and on television, to the point that tour operators in the Philippines include it in their itineraries. At present, the festival takes place on a biennial basis and is the main tourist attraction for the village, as well as the main driver for the local tourist economy.

1.2.5.2 Case study no. 2: The territory and organizational configurations: The case of the Italian Banche di Credito Cooperative

In Italy, the *Banche di Credito Cooperative*, hereinafter, cooperative banks, are pioneer institutions that provide banking services where they would otherwise not be readily available, supporting innovative individual businesses, and fostering the economic development of new communities. In contrast with a widely held belief, within their territories they are characterized by a greater ability to provide credit than other banks. The more than 400 cooperative banks that are active today constitute a significant number of credit institutions with considerable differences in terms of solidity and the capacity to respond to difficult circumstances. However, even in the most critical periods, cooperative banks have not failed to support local businesses, without losing sight of the aim of promoting local development, that is a requirement under the terms of their articles of association. Above all, they are characterized by the fact that they are territorial banks. Good management practices, the capacity to manage company processes and proper relations with the territory are widespread qualities within the category. They are at the basis of a business model in which the values of solidarity and mutual support do not act as a brake on development, but rather supplement and reinforce the balance and the solidity of the institutions. Cooperative banks have undergone a process of transformation over the past 10 years, consisting in particular of the merger of different banks that thus become subsidiaries of larger groups. This has given rise to significant economic opportunities, but also difficulties in maintaining relations with their customer base. The response to problems of this kind has taken place by means of two types of reorganization.

The first consists of the setting up of a system of entrepreneurial associations as part of a network linking a variety of institutions with a view to underlining the specific nature of the mission, the organizational model and the distinctive culture of the cooperative banks.

The second, which has a more significant impact on the various cooperative banks and their relations with the territory, depends on the organization at central level of management systems, such as Corporate Social Responsibility (CSR) audits and mission statements, which are intended to stimulate the ability of each institute to specify and communicate its social function within its territory. This results in an institutional instrument that disseminates knowledge about and promotes actions for developing the territory adopted by each individual cooperative bank. The question arises as to whether a means of communication can provide the opportunity to reconfigure the design of the organization. In many cases it can do so, taking account of the guiding principle, the recognition of the identity of each territory and also of local needs. It is not the CSR audit in itself that performs a strategic function, but rather the consistency of this statement with the objectives of territorial development. It is not possible to adopt abstract and generic programmes that are valid in all contexts, but rather those that reflect the identity of the territory, with its own specific needs. It is therefore possible to speak of a significant opportunity taken up by certain institutions as a means of promoting relations, and engaging in consultation with the local community. A number of cooperative banks have set up local committees, appointing volunteers and bank representatives responsible for social programme management, consulting the local community, and identifying and selecting development projects put forward by the community, and thus taking preference, that are necessary and useful for territorial growth. Essentially, the banks extend their organizational confines across the territory, envisaging a form of joint management of development services. As a further outcome, the function of CSR reporting leads to further changes in the organizational structure in two different ways. Many cooperative banks, in an awareness of the importance of the function of social communication, have set up a specialized department, whereas others have hired experts in CSR reporting. This results in further changes to the organizational configuration, ensuring that the banks continue to be firmly rooted in the territory.

1.2.5.3 Case study no. 3: Leading territorial development: Territorial networks across Europe

The acronym LEADER comes from the French, *Liaison entre Actions de Développement de l'Économique Rurale*, linking development actions in the rural economy. The LEADER approach constitutes one of the most important instruments devised by the European Commission for the development of rural areas, first of all as a Community Initiative Programme, and more recently as the Rural Development Programme 2021–2025. This approach was introduced due to the failure of traditional policies to deal with the problems facing many rural areas in Europe. The basic idea is to mobilize the energy and resources of the population and the local organizations as active subjects rather than as beneficiaries, enabling them to contribute to the future development of their respective rural regions, by setting up partnerships known as Local Action Groups, at territorial level involving public bodies, private-sector firms and civil society actors.

Combining the four elements of the LEADER programme (strategic priorities, the nature of the projects, the type of subjects involved, and the socio-economic resources involved, practical experience, particularly in the regions of Central and Eastern Europe), has resulted in a proliferation of locally coordinated models of networks characterized by considerable heterogeneity. Selecting a strategic objective[2] is the first major response to the various needs at territorial level. Undoubtedly the most interesting aspect concerns the model of local coordination among the actors involved in rural development initiatives. The heading "action group" is intended to indicate any form of local partnership to be constructed, taking account of the local representatives interested in the design and implementation of local strategies, decision-making processes and the allocation of resources. From the subjective point of view, as noted above, inter-sectoral partnerships include public bodies, private companies and voluntary associations.

The models of coordination ensuing from this approach are choices made by the territory in a logical sequence bringing together needs, strategic priorities and actors, determining their roles and responsibilities. In contrast with the idea of a single social network model, basically flat with a distribution as equal as possible of roles and functions, many local partnerships have set up a hierarchical structure, assigning a more central role at times to the public actor, and at other times to a consortium of local companies that takes on a dominant position. Other models of coordination have adopted a logic of bureaucratic networks, based on contracts laying down rights and obligations, with the chance of reconsidering the organizational aspects in due course. Other organizational models are difficult to place between the two extremes of network organizations and bureaucratic structures, constituting a hybrid model between the two paradigm configurations. Essentially, the considerable degree of variation in the priorities that territories adopt, even in the presence of general shared objectives of rural development, have a major impact on the nature of the activities, on the resources chosen, and above all on the model of governance of the activities and on the implications in organizational terms (https://enrd.ec.europa.eu).

1.3 Conclusions: An integrated framework derived from organizational theory

This study goes beyond the existing literature to outline an integrated theoretical framework casting light on how and under what circumstances firms interact with the territory.

Let us now attempt to summarize the analysis, bringing together the organizational dimension and the concept of territory on the basis of the following line of reasoning. The main points of this section take the arguments outlined in the previous sections and examine them from the point of view of a series of relevant questions. The question arises as to the circumstances in which the territory and the organizational dimensions interact, the nature of this interaction (either active or passive), the advantages and disadvantages. In this way, we attempt an analysis of the relationship between the firm and the territory that is in line with the definition of the territory adopted, that is, on the basis of the above discussion, as a distinct unit of analysis, a set of relations based on market dynamics as well as social interaction, and finally an environment capable of exerting influence, that is at the same time subject to influence, producing both positive and negative effects. We need to develop the discussion on the basis of these theoretical assumptions, as a conceptual framework to support the following sections.

In the first place, organizational power is a natural form of interaction with the territory. Firms survive by means of commercial exchanges and thus naturally take part in power relations, since the exercise of power defines the role played within the exchange relationship. The exercise of organizational power is a natural form of interaction with the territory. Power exercised in a territorial exchange relationship takes place in every instance in which the firm receives and exchanges resources within the territory. Territorial exchanges present advantages as they are enhanced by the social and geographic proximity of the parties, and as a result they can be easily implemented at a reasonable cost of procurement of materials, while also being easier to manage, with higher levels of trust that derive from shared cultural norms. The exercise of power by both the parties (on the part of the firm in relation to the territory, and on the part of the territory in relation to the firm), although self-evidently asymmetrical, should not result in the abuse of power by either party. However, the power intrinsic to a territorial exchange that is inequitable may be deleterious to the power exercised in a non-territorial relationship, due to the high risk of resource dependency of one party in relation to the other.

Organizational configurations are subject to variation due to the specific characteristics of different territories. A firm that operates in different territories may reconfigure its operations to respond more immediately to territorial requirements. The type of organizational configuration is thus influenced by the territory, while it is less likely for the organizational configuration to influence the territory, except in terms of micro-organizational planning, in which a specific employment grade within the organization may be replicated across the territory, with an impact on the local employment market. The positive implications consist of a higher level of compliance by the firms in relation to the characteristics of the territory. The negative implications may concern the fact that the response to territorial needs is not necessarily legal. The structural configuration results in a neutral instrument capable of having an impact on the territory that may be legal or illegal.

Territorial and corporate culture naturally depend on each other, in a manner that is almost essential. The advantages are those of social proximity: shared values result in some cases in the territory influencing the firm, and in other cases in the firm influencing the territory.

In general, a virtuous cycle is set off in which the positive effects of both processes feed into each other. The advantages concern the territorial dimension with a growth in social and occupational capital and more in general, territorial development. With regard to the firm, the absorption of local culture implies a complete recognition on the part of the territory and a strengthening of the sense of belonging to the local community. Negative implications arise in connection with illegal practices, on the part both of the firm and the territory. The reasoning is the same in both cases. The domino effect of a mutual contribution appears to be identical. The effect of a vicious cycle between the corporate culture and the territorial culture tends to act as a brake on territorial development.

In this connection, Table 1.3 provides an overview of the conceptual framework.

Table 1.3 Outline of a conceptual framework

	Reason	*Nature of the relationship*	*Positive effects*	*Negative effects*
Organizational power/territory	Inherent to territorial exchanges	Bidirectional	Advantages of geographical and social proximity	Resource dependency/ specific investments
Organizational configurations/ power	Diversity of interaction due to territorial heteroge-neity	Mainly one-directional (the territory influencing the firm)	Coherence between the structure and the territory Capacity to respond to territorial changes	Coherence between the structure and the territory (negative inputs) Capacity to respond to territorial changes (illegal practices)
Cultural organization/ territorial culture	Continuous interaction due to social proximity	Bidirectional, mutual	Recognition, sense of belonging/ identity	Recognition, sense of belonging/identity albeit illegal

Notes

1 These dimensions do not fully encompass the set of instruments by means of which interactions between the firm and the environment can be characterized but they are the most significant for the purposes of the present study.

2 The strategic objectives consist of the following: (1) improving the quality of life including the reconstruction of villages, and investment in the construction of public structures; (2) improving regional competitiveness by supporting the diversification of rural activities, both agricultural and non-agricultural, and the development of small and medium-sized firms; (3) protecting and promoting the natural environment and local culture; (4) supporting rural tourism.

2 Positive implications of the relationship between the firm and the territory

2.1 Introduction

This section begins with an overview of the next part, considering the main positive implications of the relationship between the firm and the surrounding area, in terms of territorial identity, territorial resilience and territorial sustainability. In each respect the main organizational dimension is examined, as well as the theoretical framework. In considering "focal firms", we rely on structural contingency theory, according to which there is no "one best way". In considering interactions with other actors within the territory, we rely on insights from neo-institutional isomorphism theory, viable systems theory and organizational field theory.

2.1.1 The relationship between the firm and the territory: The organizational framework

In the previous section, we carried out an in-depth examination of the relationship between the firm and the territory, focusing on the means that firms employ to develop and strengthen this relationship.

In this section, we consider another aspect to further develop the analysis. The key question here is: Under what circumstances does the firm use its organizational dimension to interact with the territory? Two key concepts were explored in the first section leading to the identification of the theoretical frameworks. They can complete the investigation of the relationship between the firm and the territory, looking beyond the resources adopted to the reasons that justify the use of organizational resources. In this view, the territory has a value as a contextual environment, making it an important site of engagement for understanding the dynamics of the firm within a given physical location.

According to this conceptualization, the territory functions as an institutional environment with its own actors defining "the rules of the game" at local level, such as local firms (Aarikka-Stenroos & Ritala, 2017; Autio et al., 2014; Vargo et al., 2015). The frameworks are chosen based mainly on whether the study focuses on the firm as the primary agent, or whether it considers the collective dimension of a number of actors, including the firm, identified within the confines of the territory.

DOI: 10.4324/9781003365075-3

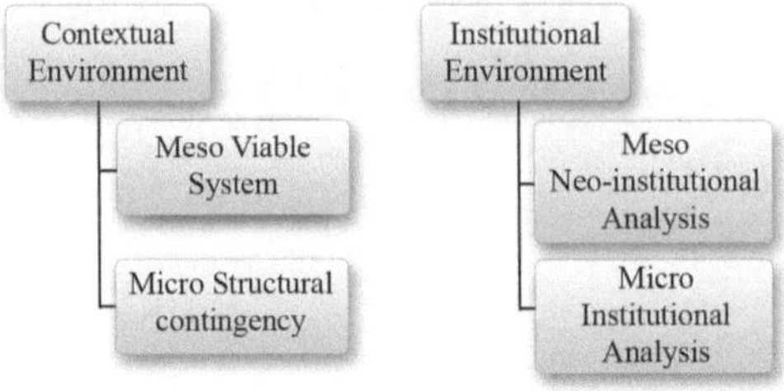

Figure 2.1 The contextual and institutional environment.

As a result, we reflect on the circumstances in which a particular firm interacts with the territory in accordance with its organizational dimensions, while on the other hand we consider the circumstances in which a group of actors, including firms, construct networks taking advantage of the conditions of proximity that the territory affords. Figure 2.1 provides an overview of the theoretical frameworks based on the nature of the environment and the level of analysis.

2.1.1.1 The contextual environment, the micro level and contingency theory

Contingency theory is based on the theoretical assumption that the optimal alignment of internal organizational factors and external conditions will improve organizational performance. In the initial theoretical conceptualizations, the organizational dimension most affected by change was considered to be the structure. The right "organizational fit" makes it possible to take advantage of key dimensions of design and technology to respond quickly to environmental changes (Otley, 2016). The subsequent theoretical evolution was based on two organizational paradigms, known as mechanistic and organic, providing different responses to various types of environmental input (Burns & Stalker, 1961). Mechanistic structures are characterized by hierarchy, centralization and task specialization, whereas organic structures are characterized by flexibility and shared responsibility between tasks. In general, organic models find the most efficient fit in turbulent and unpredictable environments. Organizations facing stable environments and predictable technologies, on the other hand, benefit from a mechanistic organizational structure in which decision-making is centralized and activities are stable over time.

Over the past 20 years, the number of studies using contingency theory to deal with the structure/environment relationship has increased, with the expansion of organizational responses to strategies, business models and human resource management (Jesmin & Hui, 2012; Abba et al.,

2018; Park, 2020). However, this adds little to the observations in the previous section, which examined changes relating to the need to respond to environmental pressures based on organizational configurations and the environment. It is important to carry out an analysis that extends contingency theory not only to the positive effects on the survival of the firm, but also to the positive effects on the surrounding environment. In essence, environmental inputs in the form of needs, modifications or development give rise to organizational responses with both internal and external value (Miles & Ringham, 2019). Thus, responses on the part of the firm to environmental requirements produce benefits of two kinds. This type of conceptual approach allows for a proper understanding of the positive aspects of the relationship between the firm and the territory that can add value to both.

The following analysis focuses on the resilience and sustainability of the firm. The argument put forward explains the use of the organizational dimension, primarily design and power relations to produce resilient responses in benefit to the firm and the territory, as well as to define sustainability objectives producing benefits both for the firm and the territory.

2.1.1.2 The contextual environment, the meso level and vital systems theory

According to the systems theory approach, the individual units of analysis can only be investigated within the specific socioeconomic context in which they are linked through relationships with reference to supra-systems and subsystems (Teece et al., 2016). Relationships are the means for the survival of the vital system, with a central position for the governing body determining strategies for systemic development and survival, supported by the system's own network of relationships. In the initial version, the approach placed the firm at the centre of the vital system, but it then transformed into a methodological lens through which to interpret various phenomena, such as the behaviour and dynamics of the territory as a whole. Since it is aimed at surviving, a viable territorial system should strengthen relationships and also its distinguishing characteristics in comparison with other systems (Barile & Saviano, 2018).

In this sense, the firm is a supra-system rooted in the territory by means of the resources it makes available through an incorporation process. In doing so, supra-systems interact with the governing bodies in a cooperative environment, using a guide that promotes coordination. The actors involved become partners who share development policies and objectives, strengthening their respective structural endowments in the interest of common growth. In essence, the governing body coordinates systemic units within the larger territorial system, thus strengthening the relationships on which decisions are based (Simone et al., 2018). This approach has the advantage of moving beyond the perspective of the focal firm in favour of considering a range of actors linked by common goals taking part in a series of relationships in which the firm is one of the parties involved, although playing a particularly central role. The key concepts of this framework allow for the optimization of the meso dimension of territories, as well as the network of relationships involving the actors in the achievement of systemic goals, in this case the goals of resilience and sustainability.

2.1.1.3 The institutional environment and the micro level: The role of institutions

Starting from North's seminal work (1990), institutions are viewed as laying down the rules of the game for the society in which the actors who create the rules exist. It is an extremely versatile concept, the contents of which vary greatly depending on the discipline (Kingston & Caballero, 2009). However, all definitions converge on one fundamental point: institutions govern the actors' behaviour. The definition of institutions focuses on the characteristics required for the institutions to guide and condition behaviour. In terms of content, Hodgson considers institutions to be systems of established and prevailing social rules that structure social interaction. Despite the difficulty of agreeing on a universal definition (Hodgson, 2006), Scott (1995) argues that: "Institutions consist of cognitive, regulatory, and regulatory structures and activities that provide stability and meaning to social behaviour". According to this definition, institutions are multifaceted structures that include symbolic systems, cognitive constructions, regulatory measures and regulatory processes.

This definition allows for both formal and informal practices to be included under the heading of institutions, meaning that both written and unwritten rules count as institutions. In general, institutions are defined as efficient when they have an effective ability to govern behaviour (Rodríguez-Pose, 2013). On the other hand, they are acceptable when the rules they lay down are capable of obtaining consent for measures that are not excessively burdensome or arbitrarily binding on those required to comply with the measures (You et al., 2022). This argument leads to a series of reflections on the relationship between the firm and the territory. If the ability to lay down rules governing collective behaviour is an essential part of the definition of institution, the question arises as to whether firms can act as institutions within the territory. The key organizational dimension to take into account is the business culture. The values shaping it extend beyond the confines of the organization and serve as models for the actions of other territorial actors as they are likely to be efficient and acceptable. Territorial legitimization is related to the recognition of the firm in its institutional role within the territory.

2.1.1.4 *The institutional environment and the meso level: Isomorphism and the organizational field*

The institutional environment consists of a range of actors, all of them capable of adopting rules, often in a synergistic manner. This is an important concept underpinning the definition of the organizational field, that was defined by DiMaggio & Powell (1983) in terms of "those organizations that, on the whole, constitute a recognized area of institutional life". An organizational field is made up of a relational space, a system of meanings and a set of rules. There is a shared institutional logic allowing institutional actors to work collaboratively. Recent studies have shifted the focus to the nature and effectiveness of the interaction between actors who share institutional purposes. In this sense, rather than external pressures, the activity of actors on the ground often has an impact on institutional purposes (McPherson & Sauder, 2013). As a result, two elements are required to define an organizational field. First, reference may be made to field agents, that is, agents who adhere to similar codes of conduct or values. This implies that interactions among these actors are more frequent, and tend to be characterized by higher levels of mutual trust than interactions with external actors. Second, institutional logics should be understood as organizational principles, in other words, cognitive, regulatory cultural structures governing social behaviour within the field (Troisi & Alfano, 2019).

If sufficiently widespread, field agents act in two ways. First, the actions they govern are perceived as appropriate. The degree of dissemination of practices within a group is sufficient in itself to recognize a certain value in the actions. Moreover, some studies (Besharov & Smith, 2014) illustrate how institutional logics differ in their impact on various agents in the field. The freedom of agents is greater in fields with a greater number of shared values or greater variability. Some members of a given community, usually in a marginal position, can more easily promote alternative or even conflicting modes of thinking than dominant ones in these contexts (Hinings et al., 2018) According to institutional theory, organizational fields are typically supported by a prevalent institutional logic (Durand & Thornton, 2018). This does not rule out the presence of additional factors operating in more confined spaces, such as sub-systems. The application of the concept of field to territory has the potential to be particularly fruitful. In the following, we assess its potential by considering the firm as an institutional actor among the institutional actors contributing to the formation of territorial identity.

Finally, Table 2.1 depicts the organizational approach to research questions.

2.2 Territorial identity and its institutional implications

An in-depth understanding of territorial identity requires a focus on the positive qualities that can be ascribed to a particular geographic area.

Table 2.1 The organizational approach to research questions

Topics	*Key questions*	*Theoretical framework*	*Organizational dimension*	*Nature of the relationship*	*Level*
Territorial Identity	Is the firm a territorial institution? Do the territorial institutions influence the organizational culture?	Institutional theory	Culture	Bidirectional	Micro
Territorial identity	Do territorial institutions act as in an organizational field?	Organizational field theory	Culture		Meso
Territorial resilience	What is the positive impact of organizational resilience on the territory?	Structural contingency	Power and structures	Unidirectional	Micro
Territorial resilience	How do territories respond to external challenges?	Viable system theory	Culture/power and structure		Meso
Territorial sustainability	Are sustainable choices at the level of the firm virtuous in territorial terms?	Institutional theory	Culture/power and structure	Unidirectional	Micro
Territorial sustainability	Who are the stakeholders involved in sustainable territorial objectives?	Viable system theory	Culture/power and structure	Bidirectional	Meso

Territorial identity is commonly understood as a socio-cultural boundary that distinguishes communities and their actors from other communities. This is a concept that has been widely used in geographical studies, particularly over the past two decades (Capello, 2018; Van Hauwaert et al., 2019; Panzera, 2022). Casting light on territorial identity means deviating from an exclusive focus on globalization processes. Essentially, it means giving due regard to territorial differences: on the one hand, there is a need to take account of the hypermobility of factors such as capital and labour, and on the other, a search for local conditions contributing to the economic success of businesses that are firmly rooted in their territories, and thus difficult to replicate in different contexts (Okunev, 2018). According to the research on the subject, globalization is not always a "voracious" phenomenon as it is capable of moving forward in parallel. Although it can override local identity through a wide-ranging process of standardization (production technologies, raw materials, consumer preferences), a series of "soft elements" means that territories are economic realities with their own distinctive traits and ability to survive, and their own attractiveness that resists the standardization imposed by globalization.

The concept of territorial identity brings together a number of intangible assets such as differences, specific characteristic and local values. Its definition is not unanimous: as in all cases where an attempt is made to frame a phenomenon that is indisputably relevant and elusive, conceptual reproduction is difficult. Some authors emphasize the prevailing characteristics, in terms of "similarity" among subjects belonging to the same territory, which implies differences with those who are extraneous to the territory, and "solidarity", which means attachment to place, a common factor that in the long run is transformed into a strong sense of belonging (Risse, 2002). Arguably, these two phenomena interact with one another. At its core, territorial identity feeds and is nourished by a common feeling that arises from the internalization and compliance with values, norms and common rules (Häkli & Paasi, 2018). In fact, the territory should be interpreted as a source of value creation that can only be nourished by exploiting mechanisms of local actor identification. Alternatively, some scholars define these dynamics as territorialization processes, though the logic is the same.

Territorial identities have an impact on territorialization and vice versa (Ravazzoli et al., 2019; Kato et al., 2022). Territorial identity promotes development as well as the conditions that foster ties and virtuous territorial relations. Through the territorial rooting of networks, territorialization tends to emphasize the "specificity of place". It should be understood as an "anchoring" related to cultural factors that lead to a consolidation of the sense of belonging of the local community (Crevoisier, 2004). Finally, identity is not a static but a dynamic process. Due to the ongoing interaction between the community and the inhabited space, it is influenced but not determined by historical identity (Oswin, 2020). The relationship that

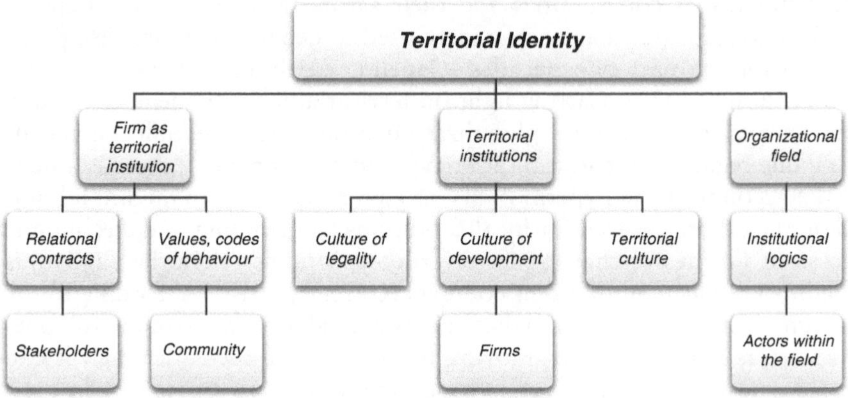

Figure 2.2 Territorial identity: Key concepts.

connects territorial identity to institutional theory emerges from this overview of studies on the subject. Identity encompasses shared values, with the result that it is local and changes over time. Consequently, a certain conceptual similarity may be perceived with the rules of the game with a territorial content. Two characteristics can be added to bring the contents of territorial identity closer to the contents of institutions: as stated above, the institution needs to be characterized by efficiency and acceptability.

The process of coalescing around common values that guide patterns of local behaviour depends on sharing, aided by the local scale of action, that is both acceptable and efficient. If there is a logical connection between the institutional rules of the game and the value models that contribute to territorial identity, the question arises about the role played by firms in the territory in a perspective that is identity-based and institutional. Can the corporate culture of a firm help to define the territorial culture? In other words, can the firm function as a local institution and shape territorial identity? Is it possible for territorial identity to have an impact on corporate culture and, as a result, corporate behaviour? Finally, if it is intended to emphasize the network of business interactions, can a collective dimension be considered?

The diagram in Figure 2.2 illustrates the key concepts of territorial identity.

2.2.1 The firm as a territorial institution

In order to understand the territorial nature of the firm, there is a need to determine whether the firm defines the rules of the game governing the relationships constructed with the territory (Taylor & Asheim, 2001). Coase's (1988) seminal definition of the firm as an institution is well known. The traditional explanation for the institutional character is that firms play an active part in a series of relationships with the environment, and they have the ability to influence the structure of economic relations. The institutional nature of firms can be clarified through a process of mental elimination. Without the firm in a given environment, the type, extent and frequency of economic interaction would take different paths than if determined by the firm itself. The firm establishes and regulates relationships. When a firm expands beyond its territorial confines, it acts as an institution in the sense that it projects its rules onto external relationships (Dicken & Malmberg, 2001). This is a useful starting point for the next part of the analysis.

The institutional component of business behaviour is reproduced on a daily basis, as it means involving external parties in production, exchange and transactions, influencing their behaviour. This involvement varies according to organizational and spatial factors. This conception of the firm builds on Penrose's (1959) theory of enterprise growth, according to which the firm is a complex institution, affecting economic and social life in many directions, encompassing many different activities, making a wide variety of meaningful decisions, influenced by a mix of unpredictable factors, but primarily governed by the logic of rationality (Penrose, 1959). However, this line of reasoning lacks the territorial characterization that the firm should exhibit when acting as a local rather than a generic institution. The institutional strength of the firm should not only be in the governance of the relational dynamics of business activities, but also in their governance within a specific space, in a particular way, according to a process of territorialization that can shape the territorial identity.

There are two strategies to consider. The first is founded on the logic of the territorially rooted firm that consolidates territorial ties including direct relationships, such as those with suppliers, distributors and local workers, that are justified for business purposes. As stated above, all daily interactions fall into this category, though they are territorially limited. The structure of imperfect contracts can be used to govern the exchange relationships that the firm sets up. They are defined in part by the national rules for the industrial sector, and in part by the rules of relational contracts. (Michler & Wu, 2020) Relational contracts provide forms of integration not necessarily specified in the contract, with rules and agreements defined by the firm. These are agreed upon by the parties as a reference framework, not actionable in a court of law, but still effective as they are based on the agreement between the parties. Relational contracts, built on a combination of formal rules and socially accepted norms, can thus represent institutional mechanisms of governance of territorial economic transactions (Argyres et al., 2020). Furthermore, as they are recognized as valid on a territorial basis, they can have a mimetic value (Woolley et al., 2022).

This means they can be replicated outside of business relationships, shaping territorially rooted business practices. Territorial characterization consists of cause and effect. On a small scale, a standard acceptance of non-contractual mechanisms of commercial relationships works well. Social proximity is the element that provides recognition and an antidote to the betrayal of non-contractual agreements, which cannot be defended in a court of law. In this way, territorialization is realized, transforming relational contracts into consolidated local practices and, in the long run, local custom.

The second strategy is less immediate than the first, but is likely to be more effective in terms of sustaining territorial identity. The firm acts as a territorial institution with regard to the community, not just in relation to the actors with whom it has commercial relations (Van der Waal & Thijssens, 2020). Through a set of values, beliefs and common goals, the firm extends the corporate culture beyond its confines. This appears to be an extremely complex process as it requires the ability to intervene outside the ordinary sphere of activity while also being effective in directing the behaviour of a community in a particular territory. However, this is a strategy that firms tend to adopt, particularly at territorial level, as firms are networks of networks, and what they normalize in their networks can easily be normalized in wider territorially defined networks. Social actors in the firm are part of specific networks in which they formulate practices to be passed on to other actors in the networks based on representation, purpose, norms and shared values (Amin & Cohendet, 2004).

It is not only business practices that can be transmitted but also values. This is likely to be a slower process, but not impossible. The most common programmes of Corporate Social Responsibility include territorial education initiatives that are consolidated by firms. It is not uncommon for businesses to seek to raise awareness in the community about safety culture, green issues and inclusiveness. These initiatives are likely to be inspired by the goal of reputational enhancement. However, it is also the case that a firm undertaking the task of guiding community behaviour requires social legitimacy in order to achieve the desired end (Moir, 2001). In this sense, an enterprise is not only a territorial institution but, more importantly, a virtuous territorial institution, as argued next in the discussion of sustainability.

2.2.2 Do territorial institutions influence organizational culture?

There are opposing points of view on this question. It has been repeatedly argued that the territory must be viewed as a unit of analysis, as a party in the relationship, rather than simply as a resource for the firm. Consequently, the relationship between a firm guided by an institutional logic and the territory is bidirectional. The firm has an impact on the territory and functions as an institution. The territory, for its part, influences the firm through its territorial institutions. The territorial assumption that influences the firm with regard to the role that territorial institutions play in the life of the firm varies according to the two types of institutions described above. On the one hand, there are formal institutions, in this case territorial institutions. On the other, there are unwritten informal institutions that are equally territorial, such as local customs, values and the connective tissue of a territory. Both are components of territorial identity, and both should be able to influence business practices. In this sense, territorial identity influences the culture of the firm and its actions through its own institutions. Territorial identity is expressed through three main strands of culture, that can have an impact on business practices, as listed next.

2.2.2.1 The culture of legality

Complying with formal rules presupposes effective institutional arrangements at territorial level. The decentralization characterizing public governance in many countries in recent years has provided an opportunity to promote certain principles with territorial implications (Kryshtanovych et al., 2020). In particular, the key institutions in the government of a territory are those closest to the public. The powers of these institutions need to be expanded as they are the most effective means of meeting local needs due to their proximity. As a result, it is up to local institutions to chart a course for community behaviour. Local regulatory measures, such as urban development plans, taxes and charges for the concession of rights on a local basis, and territorial enforcement by the courts and the local police, have an impact on the behaviour of the firm and the community (Koroso et al., 2019). The value of strong local institutions capable of promoting legality can be interpreted in negative terms. It is common to find studies pointing to the absence of a legal culture as the result of weak institutions at a local level (Troisi & Alfano, 2022a). Weak institutions regulate poorly, adopting outdated or excessively burdensome models of behaviour for the public, they coordinate in an ineffective way with law enforcement institutions, and they levy excessively high taxes to fund public services.

On the other hand, strong institutions at local level have the ability to regulate community life through measures that are up-to-date, acceptable in terms of their provisions and properly coordinated with effective law enforcement (Koroso et al., 2019) As for the relationship between firms and public institutions, the lack of certainty in terms of compliance, or regulations that are too burdensome or poorly aligned with the economic capacity of firms, tends to result in the spread of a culture of illegality. Firms that are business leaders at the territorial level seek to evade regulatory requirements or even violate them with negative externalities, particularly within the local territory. In short, firms are under pressure from public institutions to act in accordance with legal requirements. The level of influence is determined by the efficiency and legitimacy of the institutions. If local institutions are weak, a culture of illegality takes root, in which businesses play a leading role in the corruption of public officials, fraud, illegal land use and dumping of public waste, giving rise to costs with a disproportionate impact on the territories in which they operate.

2.2.2.2 *The impact of territorial institutions on the culture of development*

Territorial institutions are important in terms of local development as the link between the market and society is imbricated in the relationship between the firm and the territory, as well as the relationship between resources and how they are allocated and used. As a result of decentralization, political and administrative institutions at territorial level have a greater capacity to support the activity of firms. The culture of development is primarily determined by the interventions aimed at upgrading and promoting economic activity at territorial level, but it is also determined by the optimal selection of methods of intervention (Maddaloni, 2016). Many studies highlight the decline of development models based on the self-determination of the public authorities in favour of models of cooperation with other public and private bodies to be the main driver of territorial development (Primdahl et al., 2018; Furmankiewicz et al., 2021, Holcombe & Kemp, 2020). The introduction of territorial pacts, as well as other forms of territorial negotiation, is motivated by a logic of improved institutional efficiency. The greater the level of participation of all development actors, the more likely it is that the strategies adopted will be accepted and have a higher level of sustainability.

In addition, it is possible for the sustainability of local development strategies to be a priority for local firms, which will act accordingly. With regard to the business culture associated with a territory, as well as territories that know how to do business, reference is frequently made to the ability of the public authorities and development institutions to govern such processes. The business culture can strengthen the ability of an institution to support the economic system of a given territory. Rather than being hindered by bureaucratic procedures, firms are encouraged and supported (Schindler & Kanai, 2021). Finally, there is a mimetic effect, in the sense of a process of emulation. The actions of firms that are in line with public development policies that are sustainable over time are likely to be replicated by other firms.

2.2.2.3 *Territorial culture*

The question of territorial culture discussed above can now be examined in more detail. Territorial culture relates to the informal aspects of institutions, based on unwritten rules and local customs. As noted above, the firm is a part of the territory due to its territorial roots. Acceptance of informal rules implies both recognition of the value of these rules on the part of firms, and recognition of informal rules adopted by firms on the part of territories. At national level, many studies in the organizational literature examine the shift in human resource management based on the location of multinationals (Meyer & Xin, 2018; Obrad & Gherheş, 2018). This is the most common example because the private lives of employees always reflect on their lives at work and vice versa, and thus local traditions that shape the daily lives of workers must be considered. By way of example, reference may be made to the requirements of Ramadan for a firm employing Muslim workers, the provision of educational courses and vocational training for multinationals operating in third-world countries and the needs and traditions of the territory in which they do business. Even if we consider a more limited geographical dimension that is closer to the focus of this study, reference may be made to local customs with an impact on business operations on a territorial scale and derived from territorial culture.

To consider some specific cases, the iron and steel industry in north-eastern Italy makes use of machinery manufactured by workers with vocational skills handed down through the generations, the result of migration across Europe. Agribusinesses frequently gain a competitive advantage by combining local traditions and innovation in the manufacturing process. Typically, the production of wine, but also cheese, is based on the use of local resources and procedures that depend on local knowledge, now frequently hybridized with technologies allowing for large-scale production rather than small-scale local production.

2.2.3 Organizational field and territorial identity

A further research question to be considered concerns how to incorporate the relationship between firms and other actors in the territory into the theoretical framework of the organizational field (DiMaggio & Powell, 1983). Framing the relationship between firms and territorial agents within the organizational field entails giving territorial relations a leading role taking account not only of network dynamics, but also of institutional logic. The agents as a whole not only shape relationships, but also move within a defined area of institutional life. The space in which they act is governed by the sharing of rules, values and principles through which individually pursued goals contribute to an overall goal, which is the sum of the actions of the organizational field and its actors. The institutional logic that underpins the field has a dual value: the agents share a socio-cultural background that guides their behaviour in the same direction. By means of interaction, the agents adopt new rules derived from the institutional logic that defines the perimeter of the organizational field. In this sense, rather than external pressures, institutional strategies are frequently shaped by the agents on the ground. As noted above, two elements are required to define an organizational field. First, field agents are required, individuals who adhere to similar codes of conduct or values, implying that interactions between these subjects are more frequent and characterized by higher levels of mutual trust than interactions with external actors. Second, an institutional logic is required, that is to say, organizational principles, or cultural, cognitive and regulatory norms governing social behaviour within a given field (Troisi & Alfano, 2019).

The theoretical dimension is not the only one to highlight, as development is the most immediate concept that can cast light on the links between the organizational field, the territory and the firm. In this connection, reference is made in the literature to endogenous territorial development as a phenomenon that emerges and spreads from the bottom up, rather than from the top down (Duarte et al., 2020). This type of development consists of an autonomous local economic system governed by local actors in decision-making processes. The central feature of the model is the production on the part of the firm of social capacities in collaboration with other institutions operating in the territory and utilizing a variety of additional capacities. Local agents make use of local resources including raw materials, labour, historically accumulated capital at the local level, entrepreneurial skills and the specific knowledge of production processes. Furthermore, they have the capacity to control the process of capital accumulation, they influence the capacity for innovation, and they develop a set of productive interdependencies at local level, both within and across sectors. The production of social capacity constitutes the added value that underpins this type of development, that we can define as a shared and synergistic ability to transform the economic and social system according to its own rules. Endogenous local development is the result of collective intelligence that relies on territorial and institutional environmental factors to achieve a common goal (Gkartzios & Lowe 2019; Calabrò & Cassalia, 2017). On the basis of this logic, it is possible to imagine an organizational field as the platform that activates the drivers of collective intelligence. Local interactions are frequently framed as social capabilities and the element that governs shared action.

In an in-depth analysis, shared rules and values emerge which serve as the foundation for a shared capacity to achieve development goals. These rules lead on to for further reflection. Each endogenous development model is likely to be unique as it is the result of the transformation of territorial factors. In all probability there are as many territorial development models as there are organizational fields. The explanation is in the field rather than in the development model: its unique characteristics are determined by territorial actors who guide and implement development strategies based on local knowledge, resources and skills, as well as knowledge, values and beliefs that cannot be replicated beyond the particular field due to the specific characteristics of the territory.

2.2.4 *Case studies*

2.2.4.1 *Case study no. 1: The impact of the firm on the territory. Ferrero: From Italy to India*

The story of Ferrero may be seen as a forerunner of Corporate Social Responsibility, with a particular focus on the territory. The Ferrero brand, known all over the world for Nutella chocolate spread, is associated with a variety of capitalism in which the firm establishes strong links with the territory in which it operates, in this case, first in Italy, then globally. The firm was set up in impoverished post-war Italy in the hilly region of the Langhe. The Ferrero management did not uproot the agricultural labourers from their fields; instead, they provided a minibus service that picked up the workers in the morning and returned them to their homes in the evening. This system, characterized by the efficient management of seasonal labour, enabled Ferrero workers to continue to farm their smallholdings, resulting in a kind of pact between the firm, the territory and the workers. But in what sense can Ferrero be seen as a territorial institution? The provision of minibus services for the workers became a means of organizing and coordinating agricultural and industrial employment in parallel. It became a well-proven system that was later adopted in the factories of Baramati, India. The Ferrero development project in rural India followed the same logic as the post-war Italian development of the Langhe. In India, as in Italy 60 years before, there was a rural economy that the small farmers did not intend to abandon, but rather became an industry-driven economy. As a result, the Italian buses were replaced by Indian minibuses transporting workers at the Indian plant to and from work, giving them time to farm the land. Furthermore, the minibus system became widespread in the area because other industries, following Ferrero's example, recognized the value for the local territory of empowering the workers by enabling them to abandon the rural economy, instead considering it an important part of the organization of their lives and work.

2.2.4.2 *Case study no. 2: The impact of the firm on the territory: The culture of the gaucho and the rural economy*

Argentina has attempted to deal with the cultural tension between domestic consumption and the export of commodities by forging a shared national identity through food products. The characteristics of modern commodity production reveal the tension between these two competing needs. Due to extensive agriculture and livestock production, and with the increased use of mechanization and transport, fewer and fewer people are now required to produce a massive surplus of marketable goods. In this context, the Argentine gaucho is a symbol of the country's independence as well as a symbol of a particular mode of livestock breeding that is an important component of the country's heritage. Gauchos still herd cattle, raise sheep and brand horses as they did in the past, and they have an enviable reputation as the producers of important agricultural products. The traditional gaucho coexists with modern intensive soy farms, which occupy 18 million hectares (44 million acres) and bring in USD 6 billion per year (5.7 billion euros at the time of writing) to the Argentine economy. Argentina is the world's largest exporter of soybean oil, with large soybean farmers looking for properties even in hilly rural provinces where land is cheap but not always ideal for soya production, and cattle are typically raised in the gaucho style. Any entrepreneur who intends to set up a cattle ranch is aware that there is only one way to ensure high-quality meat production in Argentina, and it is gaucho-style ranching that survives despite the fact that it is deprived of the land for the cattle to graze freely, since in the gaucho tradition grazing is free. One option would be to make the transition to modern farming, cultivating the vast expanses of the Argentine pampas, and replace cattle ranching with modern intensive farming methods. However, entrepreneurs in Argentina who believe in quality realize that the only way to achieve it is to respect the gaucho tradition and extensive farming methods.

2.2.4.3 Case study no. 3: Organizational field and safety culture

A recent study (Troisi & Alfano, 2019) examined an organizational field in territories with a high risk of earthquakes, characterized by an institutional logic of security. The study found that the culture of safety is shared among actors within the organizational field, corresponding to the city limits. Key actors, local government authorities, construction companies, the local associations of engineers and architects and, finally, the local community were all taken into account. Local territorial authorities are responsible for enforcing safety standards in accordance with national regulations. In addition, urban planning is adopted by the local authorities for regulating land use across areas based on population density, hydrogeological characteristics and risk exposure. Construction companies were evaluated in two ways: first, on the basis of their economic and financial strength, calculating the bankruptcy rate in the areas concerned, and second, on the basis of the number of infringements for violations of safety standards in the construction industry. Professional associations operate at a local level and engage in a variety of activities, particularly short training courses, with the aim of raising awareness about safety issues among the members of the association. The number of local initiatives on health and safety education and training, and the number of cases of buildings constructed without proper planning permissions in relation to the resident population were taken as proxies for the safety culture of the local community. By means of descriptive statistics, the study demonstrated that the type of activity that indicates a given level of safety culture is homogeneous in the sense that it characterizes all or most of the actors in the field. In areas with a high seismic risk, there are three possible scenarios, as outlined next.

A high level of safety training tends to be homogeneous across territories, as shown by up-to-date municipal plans, the stability of local enterprises, low numbers of buildings without proper planning permission, a large number of education and training programmes and a sufficient number of safety training courses offered over time. The same logic applies to intermediate and lower levels that are not affected by seismic risk. Different perceptions of safety culture are to be found among the actors: the shared institutional logic does not always lead to positive outcomes. As a result, a local community may place a strong emphasis on safety while also not being fully aware of its significance. However, it is worth repeating that anyone in the field promotes a safety culture comparable to that of the other actors.

2.3 Territorial resilience: Bridging the gap between firms and system resilience

This section reviews the literature about the resilience of firms and its effects on the territory, focusing on the ability of organizations to deal with changes in the external environment. Based on insights from structural contingency theory, it discusses organizational flexibility in terms of design, power and resources. In addition, it examines how territories respond to external challenges and shocks, with firms considered as part of an ecosystem that seeks to identify collective solutions to respond to territorial needs and capacities. Finally, two case studies are presented examining the resilience of the firm, and system resilience in times of COVID-19.

2.3.1 Resilience as a complex but positive concept

Resilience is a complex phenomenon (Frigotto et al., 2022), and it is important to link the resilience of the firm to that of the territory. This gives rise to the need for an in-depth examination of the positive impact of the relationship between the firm and the territory. The fundamental idea is that the firm can act as the primary actor in territorial initiatives by deploying appropriate resources to respond to unexpected events. This argument is supported by the theoretical framework of structural contingency, which states that an unexpected external pressure is a contingent stimulus that the firm needs to interpret in order to identify responses that are not only immediate but also effective. The effectiveness needs to be twofold: the firm must know how to devise a response in the immediate aftermath of the event, and how to plan a response that places it in the conditions that existed prior to the shock event (Song et al., 2022). As previously stated, structural contingency theory considers the positive effects of organizational responses not only in terms of the exclusive benefits for the firm, but also of the positive externalities that the firm produces within the territory.

This is the key to understanding the further development of the topic, beyond the indirect benefits that resilient businesses bring to a territory. It extends to casting light on how the firm can act as the key agent in terms of territorial responses, which are put in place in conjunction with other agents in the wake of unexpected events. The effects of unexpected events are not limited to the impact on a particular business, but also to the impact on the territory as a whole. Furthermore, the concept of resilience can be framed through two understandings of effectiveness. It is a concept that has gained interdisciplinary attention in recent decades, making the transition from a narrow application in the hard sciences to a wider application in the social sciences (Linkov & Trump, 2019). It appears to be difficult to find a synonym for this expression. Resistance is insufficient, since resilience indicates an attempt to identify long-term responses as well as immediate responses to an unexpected event (Pike et al., 2010). The difficulty of finding an equivalent term is primarily due to its complexity, particularly in its application in the social sciences.

A significant number of studies in the social sciences, in particular, highlight the complexity of resilience in terms of the dimensions involved. In theory, there is widespread agreement that a complex problem cannot be dealt with a piecemeal approach. Many studies focus on particular dimensions of resilience pertaining to communities, networks or organizations, overlooking the fact that these dimensions are frequently interconnected (Weick & Sutcliffe, 2007). Organizational resilience, as discussed next, is commonly defined as the ability to deal with structural changes and human resources (Lampel et al., 2014). This gives rise to the need for adaptability and vulnerability in order to respond in a sustainable manner. The distinction is often made between operational resilience, meaning the ability to recover after a crisis, and strategic resilience, the ability to turn threats into opportunities (Ruiz-Martin et al., 2017). The concept of network resilience concerns "the ability to withstand a drop in network performance and take action to restore it to a desired level" (Ramirez-Marquez et al., 2018).

The human component of community resilience is the focus of a number of studies, as part of the recovery phase, particularly at the local level. "The emphasis of human resilience is on processes that improve people's ability to recover from disasters as quickly as possible with little or no outside help. This approach recognises that communities have developed certain levels of resilience over time. Local adaptation strategies, culture, heritage, knowledge, and experience are critical components in promoting disaster resilience" (Sorokin, 1942). Some studies have attempted to identify the determinants of territorial resilience and the number of agents operating in a resilient manner, with firms always playing a key role. However, it is essentially a numerical matter: the more firms that are rooted in a territory, the more they can form networks and, as a result, the more likely it is that the economic consequences of an external shock can be absorbed. The network of firms allows for the rapid dissemination of the know-how required to

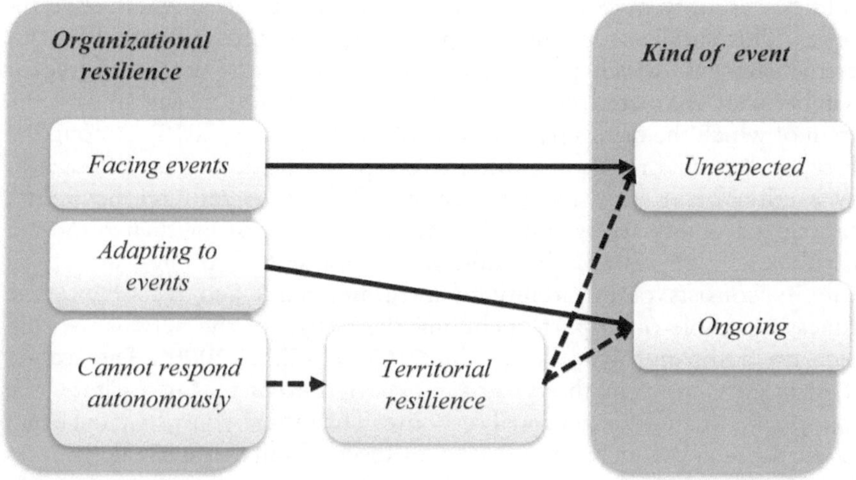

Figure 2.3 Resilience: Key concepts.

develop crisis responses. As a result, the territory discovers an important collective dimension in network responses (Brunetta et al., 2019).

Others scholars argue that the response lies not only in the ability of a network of firms, but also in the integration of economic networks with social networks (Berkes & Ross, 2013). Another strand of research broadens the resilience of the territory to the ability of firms, research centres and institutions to devise shared strategies. At the very least, these agents are required to adopt joint strategies, while fostering links with a variety of other participants (Ramirez-Marquez et al., 2018). In the following, the focus will be on the resilience of the firm, considered as a micro response in which the reconfiguration of organizational factors facilitated by organic models is central. The focus then moves to resilience with a territorial dimension, relating to the collective ability of a territory to respond to unexpected events, arguing that the two dimensions intersect.

The diagram in Figure 2.3 illustrates the key concepts of resilience.

2.3.2 *The resilience of firms as organizational resilience*

When it comes to organizational resilience, there are three major lines of inquiry. The first line of inquiry is concerned with efforts to develop an autonomous concept of resilience based on the organizational dimensions through which a resilient response is implemented. It is widely agreed that organizational resilience should be defined as the ability of an organization (firm) to recover from an internal or external shock and ideally to return to pre-shock status (e.g. Vogus & Sutcliffe, 2007). In this sense, structural contingency theory suggests that organizations that can address environmental uncertainty quickly are the ones that devise the most effective responses. This entails providing a response based on the ability to adapt to external changes, which is recognized in the literature as the degree of flexibility that characterizes the organization, first and foremost, and the system of which the firm is part (Baškarada & Koronios, 2018). Among the sub-types identified in the literature, two types of flexibility are believed to play a critical role in resilient responses. The first is resource flexibility, meaning the ability to dynamically redistribute and strengthen resources (Onyokoko et al., 2021). In addition to resource flexibility, structural flexibility consists of the ability to integrate, build and reconfigure the business in whole or in part, including the design of the network within which the company operates (Verdu & Gómez-Gras, 2009). The second line of inquiry concerns the type of unexpected event that necessitates the development of an organizational response. The most frequently cited event is a shock, which is defined as a case of discontinuity or a break with an existing technological, organizational or market situation (Altinas & Royer, 2009). The shock may be an economic crisis, a natural disaster or, in the current situation, a health emergency. Otherwise, it is an event that takes the form of a continuous process of change in the contextual and institutional environment of the firm (Nelson et al., 2007). This may mean technological innovation, changes in consumer preferences and expectations or a shift in market dynamics. In this context, the ability of the firm to reinvent business models to respond to the needs of globalized markets is crucial. In any case, resilience is required. With one exception: the time difference between two types of events.

When an unexpected event occurs, the firm needs to reinvent itself. The greater the flexibility afforded by organic models, the greater its ability to respond quickly and effectively. In the case of an ongoing event, the response corresponds to a much longer-term change process that can lead to more radical changes in the structural design of the firm. In short, the first type of resilience concerns the immediate response of firms and flexibility, whereas the second type does not require an immediate response and involves more profound changes that are only marginally characterized by organizational flexibility

The third line of inquiry concerns the nature of the unexpected events and distinguishes between two types of responses. In the first case, the firm needs to resist. In the second, the events are gradually incorporated into the firm's decisions because, in the case of long-term events, the firm is less concerned with limiting the immediate effects and more concerned with adapting to ongoing changes in order to capitalize on the opportunities. Adopting a certain degree of flexibility or initiating more profound changes will be dependent on the particular skills of the firm. These will enable the firm to face shocks or pressure from environmental factors that cause others to fail and go out of business. More specifically, they are the distinct skills that generate an ability for immediate learning from the unexpected event, resulting in the re-use of knowledge, procedures, rules and operating methods. Essentially, firms adopt these technical and organizational responses to limit damage and reconfigure operations in response to emerging needs (Baghersad & Zobel, 2022).

Gilly et al. (2014) examine organizational resilience by identifying three possible models of resilient behaviour. According to the first model, firms face a long-term event and implement a radical change process, having the necessary skills and learning processes to make choices that not only limit the effects of the event but also capitalize on the opportunities. According to the second model, firms face a sudden and unexpected event, responding quickly and in flexible ways, allowing them to mitigate the effects, again thanks to their specific skills. According to the third model of behaviour, firms are unable to respond to an event regardless of its duration. They compensate for their inability to respond autonomously by cooperating as members of local networks affected by the unexpected event. In addition to complementary skills, what matters in this case is the level of trust among the actors, common representations, shared rules and similar values (Colletis, 2010). Territorial resilience appears to be the most appropriate approach to collective resilience.

2.3.3 Territorial resilience

The conditions that need to be met to identify the phenomenon of territorial resilience are as follows: first, the localized nature of the event, that could be a large-scale event, but the consequences must vary by territory; second, the impact on the economy of the territory; third, the presence of local institutions, both formal and informal (Brunetta et al., 2019). The territorial resilience that emerges as a result of these conditions is thus specific to a territory, along with its capacity to adapt. The ability of firms and the territory as a whole to adapt to changes and shocks is unlikely to be replicated across territories. Regaining dynamism and charting a new course after major disruption requires looking to the past and present, identifying the strengths and weaknesses of the territory, and projecting it into the future. On closer inspection, territorial resilience complements the third model of behaviour identified above (3.2). It is the result of the collective action of the territorial actors, including firms, who devise a response to external events, whether a sudden crisis or a significant change in the productive and technological context. This concept of territorial resilience is linked to a particular definition of the territory. The conditions of proximity incorporated in the concept of territory adopted in this study are necessary for a collective response that is also resilient.

A pre-existing network of relationships is required for a resilient response. It is difficult to imagine a network constructed to reduce the impact of an unexpected event on a large scale without agents who share common spaces for action. There must be technological proximity, social proximity and, of course, geographical proximity. The territory is a natural location for relationships of trust: the network should not be tested in an emergency, but rather strengthened by such an event. The territory is a natural location for geographical proximity. Clearly, geographical proximity facilitates face-to-face interaction and thus allows for exchanges. Face-to-face communication, in particular, enables the dissemination and recombination of various kinds of knowledge and reduces participant opportunism (Boschma, 2005). According to Kechidi & Talbot (2010), face-to-face communication enables the participants to address and solve new problems that none of the participants acting in isolation would be able to face. The territory, as a synthesis of such proximity, constitutes a potential that, when activated by the interaction of the participants, reproduces a resilient response for the benefit of individual actors, with the added benefit of a multiplier effect for the territory (Gilly & Torre, 2000). At this point, the question arises as to why firms should play such an important role in creating a resilient network.

Essentially, they serve as key agents in the transmission of knowledge, and thus in the technological proximity required for defining a resilient response. The network can function as a result of social proximity. Geographic proximity enables firms to function more effectively. However, these are factors that optimize the connections between the actors but have a limited impact on the activities in terms of their content. Dealing with an unexpected event requires specific knowledge and, above all, the ability to disseminate that knowledge. In this regard, firms undoubtedly play an important role. Any event that may affect a territory, whether it be an economic shock or a health emergency, gives rise to the need for solutions that require know-how, the implementation of operational models and the identification of routines, all of which are in most cases decided by firms. A case in point is COVID-19. Although it was and continues to be a health emergency, it was up to pharmaceutical companies to seek treatments and safe and effective vaccines, utilizing a wide range of scientific and technical skills. In a different, but equally important, way, it is up to firms to seek to maintain business as usual even when local lockdowns have halted most business operations. The continuity of economic activity has allowed territories to survive and produce wealth despite the ongoing difficulties (Troisi & Alfano, 2021). When we speak of technological proximity, we are referring to behavioural models in which the contribution of know-how in a broad sense is indispensable.

As in the case of public health emergencies, economic crises show that the business models that firms adopt to deal with critical events is based on a specific understanding of how to overcome a crisis, which is beneficial to many actors. As a result, they can be transferred to other firms as well as public bodies through technological proximity. Territorial resilience is a collective response in which firms play an important but not exclusive role, as the crisis gives rise to the need for the participation of other actors.

Territorial resilience places the firm at the centre of the network due to its ability to be a technological proximity actor: the complementary nature of the actors' skills and abilities facilitates the development of relationships in response to the event, strengthened by bonds of social proximity and spatial and geographical contiguity. Faced with a new problem, the actors collaborate in a stable manner to identify new responses (technical, organizational and relational) and new forms of territorial governance, as part of a process of territorial resilience.

2.3.4 Case studies

2.3.4.1 Case study no. 1: Non-profit organizations, COVID-19 and resilience

The public health emergency due to the spread of COVID-19 and the restrictions on daily life that became necessary in the early months of 2020 affected the entire world, resulting in the halting of productive activities in a large number of firms and radically altering individual lifestyles and consumption habits. Non-profit organizations constitute an emblematic case of territorial resilience in such scenarios where the virus has been the driving force behind the increase in poverty and inequality. They have been able to transform the local community, sometimes dramatically, to carry on their activities and remain active protagonists and provide essential services for their users and the territories in which they operate, always at the forefront of the emergency response. Consequently, social enterprises deserve attention for being resilient far beyond the ability to adapt quickly. The resilience of non-profit organizations all over the world at the height of the COVID-19 pandemic has led to a creative rethinking of their activities and services without disregarding their social mission or economic goals. As a result, the many stories of resilient non-profit organizations at the height of the pandemic share certain characteristics. They are primarily concerned with flexibility in dealing with the crisis, manifested in three main ways. On the one hand, their activities needed to be reconfigured in many cases. This reconfiguration, frequently resulting in the digital provision of services previously provided in person, has enabled organizations to ensure, as far as possible, continuity in the provision of services, which is critical particularly for user groups such as people who are chronically ill, people with disabilities and older people.

The second means of delivery has involved the activation of new services or products through the conversion of production lines and organizational activities. The adaptability of production processes has enabled the expansion of services, human resources and economic resources to meet the increasing fragility and emerging needs caused by the pandemic. As an example, during the first wave of the health emergency, some non-profit bodies in the textile sector began producing reusable masks. In addition, various organizations have launched psychological support services online and by phone for their users or anyone who feels the need to talk. Moreover, many residential facilities for elderly and disabled people, in addition to reconfiguring procedures in the interests of health and safety, have made available their own premises and staff to support hospitals overwhelmed by COVID-19 patients within a short timeframe. The question arises as to why territorial resilience in relation to COVID-19 has put non-profit organizations in the spotlight. There appear to be two main reasons: the strong rooting of social enterprises and other third-sector entities in the territory in which they operate, and the contact they have established with their communities as a result of this close bond.

In short, social, geographical and, not least, technological proximity are still at work. During the first wave of the health emergency, social enterprises were able to capitalize on relationships established and cultivated over time with the general public and other actors in the territory, becoming an even more important service provider for the community.

These skills and characteristics of third-sector bodies are frequently not given due recognition by public-sector bodies that are geographically close but perceived as socially distant. In this connection, mention should be made of the importance of the technological proximity of non-profit bodies to their users, which lies in their ability to identify and respond quickly to the needs of their communities, even when emerging needs arise. In summary, a model of flexible organization, which is the foundation for effective and rapid decision-making, has given rise to a resilient response. Thanks to their proximity and knowledge of their communities, non-profit organizations have emerged as key actors in implementing a broader and more complex territorial resilience.

2.3.4.2 *Case study no. 2: Healthcare providers and COVID-19: The Italian experience: Hospitals, networks and territorial adaptability*

One of the major challenges posed at the height of the pandemic was the simultaneous management of two types of hospital demand: first, COVID-19 patients, those given priority around the world over the last 2 years, and second, non-COVID-19 patients, those whose conditions typically result in hospitalization, as either acute or chronic patients. The problem that concerned the response of the health service at one point was finding time, resources and the means to balance emergency healthcare management with day-to-day management, in order to avoid irreversible harm to patients suffering from conditions other than COVID-19. Numerous reports have highlighted the difficulty of gaining access to hospitals for this category of patients all over the world for two reasons. First, hospitals were inundated with COVID-19 cases, particularly at the height of the pandemic, and second, there was a risk that non-COVID-19 patients would be more easily infected due to their increased vulnerability.

Several studies have found that the resilience of healthcare providers (particularly hospitals) is a significant expression of territorial resilience. There are three reasons for this. The first reason is that they are fully fledged organizations with deep roots in the community, as they primarily respond to the needs of the territory where they are located. Due to the functions they perform, they are part of an institutional network of territorial actors that includes the local government, universities and other smaller healthcare providers. The second reason is that hospitals have responded to the COVID-19 emergency based on the number of cases of infection in the territory, with emergency responses varying from one territory to another. The third reason is that where the territorial health network has been effective, it has allowed for the management of the emergency, striking a balance between the demands of the two categories of hospital patients.

According to some studies, virtuous cases of territorial resilience to the COVID-19 emergency relied on the use of flexibility both at the hospital and network level. Hospital flexibility was primarily defined by resource flexibility, relating to the internal ability of healthcare providers to combine human and instrumental resources, whereas external flexibility concerns the organizational reconfiguration of the network, strengthening certain healthcare providers and, in some cases, activating new network links. It has also been demonstrated that balancing the internal resources of hospitals in order to provide equal access to both categories of patients was achieved by implementing flexibility processes (including both tangible and intangible assets, and human resources) and learning processes requiring a medium-term perspective. Network flexibility, that is primarily required to smooth the overall flow of patients in hospitals, has been leveraged and proven to work by improving decentralized services, particularly for patients not in a critical condition, and by utilizing telemedicine. In essence, network resilience works well if it has previously been implemented, whereas new agreements put in place at the height of the COVID-19 pandemic did not work well due to the low level of social and technological proximity of actors dealing with a major public health emergency for the first time.

2.4 Sustainability choices: The role of firms and territorial stakeholders

This section examines the concept of sustainability within a specific territory. In an institutional theory perspective, it seeks to explain why decisions about sustainability at the level of the firm give rise to the need for the structural reconfiguration of production, as well as changes in the corporate culture, that often turn out to be virtuous in territorial terms. In terms of viable system approach, the need for the participation of a wide range of stakeholders at territorial level places the firm at the centre of a network achieving sustainability objectives by means of a collective effort. Finally, two case studies are examined to show how territorial sustainability and the sustainability of the firm can work together to mutual advantage.

2.4.1 The concept of sustainability: The links between development and the territory

Many sustainability studies, attempting to provide a common definition, refer to the Brundtland Report (1987) by the World Commission on Environment and Development: "Sustainable development is far from being a definitive condition of harmony, it is rather the process of change, that the exploitation of resources, the direction of investments, the orientation of technological development and institutional changes are made consistent with future needs as well as with the current ones". This definition gives rise to the concept of economic sustainability, which is widely understood as the ability to allocate the available resources efficiently by imposing a fundamental constraint that has always existed but is now more evident than ever: resources are scarce by definition. As a result, resources cannot be allocated in a way that is wasteful and harmful in the long run. The concept of social sustainability is then added, defined as the ability to ensure conditions of stability, justice and democracy by understanding the need for factors of well-being (safety, health, education) to be equitably distributed across classes and genders. Finally, environmental sustainability means the ability to maintain natural resource quality and reproducibility. Since these are overlapping dimensions, sustainability goals rarely focus on just one.

This is especially important for this study since it clarifies two considerations that are fundamental. The first one, based on the concept of overlapping dimensions, is the importance of the intersection between sustainability and development. By combining economic and social issues, economic and environmental objectives and environmental and social sustainability, development dimensions that have traditionally been viewed as complementary can be dealt with. The second consideration is that sustainability or sustainable development necessarily concerns actions within specific boundaries since environmental, economic and social issues vary greatly across geographical areas. It is not always necessary to frame them as national issues: there is a geo-spatial dimension for sustainability that is decentralized in administrative terms, frequently coinciding with the regions. In a broader sense, sustainability is a matter for territories, since the aims of sustainable development frequently overlap with those of territorial development, particularly in relation to the social environment and the economy. Based on the observations in the previous sections about the characteristics of the territory, sustainability is by definition an integrated phenomenon aimed at maintaining a certain standard of living for the community and improving its quality through the effective use of the economic, social and natural resources of the territory.

In support of the argument that sustainability finds it natural collocation in territories, consider that the various tools for evaluating sustainability actions in the literature always include the territory as the subject of evaluation. Evaluation based on classification systems consists of comparative surveys of territorial ecosystems (Córdova et al., 2018), whereas the principles-based approach focuses on monitoring in line with the principles of sustainability and development in specific territorial ecosystems (Simeonova et al., 2009). Another critical issue for understanding territorial sustainability strategies is the perspective from which the investigation is conducted.

Two distinct perspectives are relevant here, which are frequently used in isolation. The first perspective focuses on the systemic approach. The various dimensions of sustainability represent the configuration of a system, and thus an expression of the complex network of components, relationships and active interactions required for the pursuit of complex objectives. Creating optimal system conditions entails putting the theoretical principles of sustainable development into practice through participatory processes extended to a number of actors, the degree of intervention varying according to the specific territory. In this connection, the World Bank defines sustainable development as a portfolio of activities aimed at preserving and expanding people's opportunities (Pavolová et al., 2019). The most important facets of sustainable development are ecology, technology and the quality of life. In the face of emerging political, technological and environmental challenges, these strategic directions encourage the search for management resources and mechanisms for implementation at territorial level. These activities result in the involvement of multiple actors, the nature of which depends on the strategic priorities, which are defined on a contingent basis considering the characteristics of a specific territory as part of the process of sustainable development.

According to the second perspective, firms are seen as crucial players in territorial development. The reason for this is that the necessary condition for an effective use of resources is a paradigm shift at the economic level, that is primarily the responsibility of firms (Ryszawska, 2018). A wide range of factors within the firm are drivers of sustainable development. Economic growth may be defined as the creation of value for firms, the ability to generate employment levels on a sustainable basis and the long-term growth of living standards and prosperity for people along this path. Further factors include resource efficiency through green technologies, the reduction of the environmental impact and the broader theme of the circular economy (Balkyte & Tvaronaviiene, 2010). All these concepts can be traced back to Corporate Social Responsibility. The following discussion examines these perspectives. On the one hand, firms are regarded as key actors of sustainability in the sense that any change in the economic paradigm that is intended to be implemented produces additional benefits for the territory. On the other, firms operate within networks, that are necessary to achieve territorial sustainability, with varying degrees of success due to the priorities that each particular territory assigns to sustainability (Figure 2.4).

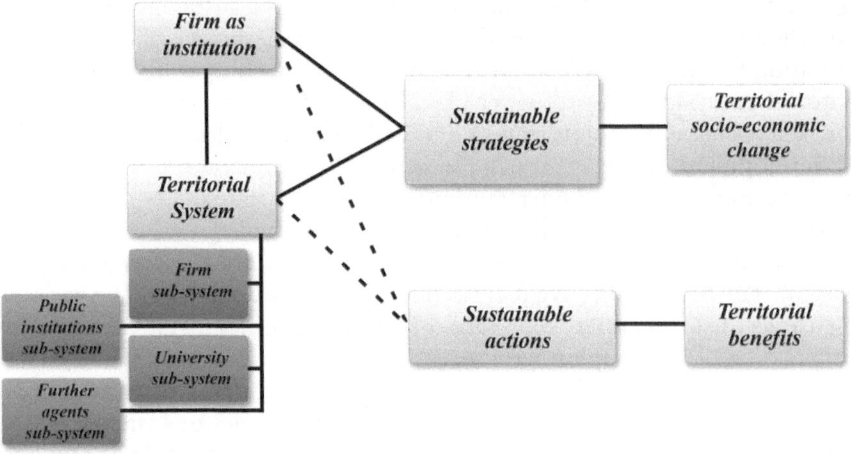

Figure 2.4 Sustainability: Key concepts.

2.4.2 *The sustainable choices of firms and the impact on the territory: The institutional perspective*

One important strand of the literature, both development and managerial in nature, considers the firm to be the key agent of sustainability. Many expressions have been coined to describe entrepreneurs who use their resources in accordance with a logic of sustainability, without sacrificing the goal of profit. Some scholars refer to them as eco-entrepreneurs (e.g. Kummitha, 2020), others as responsible entrepreneurs (Choi & Gray, 2008) and still others as firms that drive sustainability (De las Heras-Rosas & Herrera, 2020). They share the concept of an entrepreneur who, in contrast with the traditional entrepreneur, prioritizes the needs of the community over profit maximization, contributing in various ways to improving the quality of life in the community. In sustainability-based entrepreneurship, the private firm becomes a vehicle to improve environmental quality and social well-being, while ensuring business survival. Financial profitability may be considered to be a means of achieving both individual and group goals (Tilley & Parrish, 2006), while changing the economic paradigm can have far-reaching consequences for sustainability. The most common sustainability strategy involves the entrepreneur's ability to modify production processes to reduce their environmental impact, with immediate consequences for the territory.

However, the firm has numerous opportunities to be a key player in sustainability by improving aspects that are both individual and collective in order to produce additional benefits for the community in the territory where it is located. Adopting strategies that primarily involve human resource management practises aimed at improving the well-being of workers, such as respecting and promoting work-life balance, constitutes a shift in the economic paradigm. Applying equitable incentive distribution models and inclusive actions is beneficial in terms of the welfare of the workforce. The key to social sustainability is to promote business practices that have a positive impact not only on the workers but also on the members of the community The list could grow exponentially, to include thousands of Corporate Social Responsibility measures that are frequently intended to add value to business interventions that are capable of resulting in community improvements. (Frynas & Yamahaki, 2016)

In some ways, this type of entrepreneurship appears to be similar to third-sector bodies in providing services that benefit the community (Tortia & Troisi, 2021). In addition, both types of actor fill a void left by public bodies in the provision of critical social and environmental goods and services by means of this function. However, sustainable entrepreneurs have an ability to achieve results that are similar in many ways. The key elements are to be found in the entrepreneurial dynamics of sustainability, using the market as a constant parameter. Unlike charities, sustainability entrepreneurs create opportunities in markets as a means of financing transactions and, more importantly, use the position of the firm within the market to channel market forces to support those objectives. This is a fundamental implication that, in participating in the market, captures a further function of sustainability performed by entrepreneurs (Gibbs, 2009).

A more recent body of research recognizes this type of entrepreneur as playing a dynamic role. As a result, it is not restricted to producing the advantage that results from thinking sustainably. These entrepreneurs are regarded as catalysts for a wider socioeconomic structural change (e.g. Parrish, 2009). Designing and implementing interventions with the primary goal of improving environmental quality and social well-being leads to change, constituting a model of behaviour for the institutions and the community. The benefits produced by firms for their territories can be used by regulatory institutions to promote regulatory and administrative changes. According to this idea of sustainability, such changes allow firms to continue operating in favourable institutional conditions (Quimbayo Ruiz, 2020). A firm that reduces carbon emissions can advocate the development of rules to support and encourage this type of policy, such as tax breaks or credit facilities for further changes in the process of production to reduce emissions. Simultaneously, responsible business decisions can be accepted and normalized by the community within a territory. Promoting the well-being of employees can become a long-term strategy that is emulated throughout the network in which the firm operates, first and foremost through its stakeholders and then through other networks. The territory and the advantages of proximity once again contribute to the delivery of a strategy, promoting acceptance and normalization of good practices.

The institutional theoretical approach explains the catalytic role of sustainability-driven firms (Parrish & Foxon, 2009). The firm that introduces technological change can stimulate institutional change, fuelled by the positive effects of technological changes on the target communities. The territory becomes a crucial site of engagement. In fact, the impact of benefits is primarily territorial. In most cases, changing a process means improving the surrounding environment. Local governments should be the first to be involved, either by supporting such improvements, adopting rules or facilitating sustainable choices. As a global phenomenon, devolution in the sense of the decentralization of decision-making implies a level administrative management directly attributed to local governments. The actors (municipalities, regions) that have benefitted from technological change have regulatory power. Although this is not a national regulatory power, such regulation has the advantage of being contiguous to the practical needs of communities. This is accomplished through the use of secondary standardization, which is typically the responsibility of local institutions that make rules within national frameworks based on the needs of the territory. Business activities that generate benefits must be expanded further, thanks to local regulatory administrative measures: the strategic actions of firms can reshape the institutional foundations of their businesses (Filser et al., 2019).

Sustainability entrepreneurs can act as catalysts for the structural socio-economic transition of a territory to a sustainable economy, promoting strategies that are not limited to meeting the immediate needs of consumers, but that have the ability to exert institutional pressure for stakeholders and the community as a whole. On the one hand, there are direct relationships that are justified by economic activity, such as those with suppliers, distributors and local employees. The list includes all the relations taking place on a daily basis and geographically concentrated. As stated above, the exchange relations of firms can be developed using imperfect contracts. They are defined in part by national rules of the industrial sector, and in part by relational contract rules. As argued above, relational contracts are the best route for transferring sustainability practices. On a territorial level, the dynamic is simpler because agents can test the value of the paradigm changes that the firm has achieved, and comply with them, to the extent that individual agents are capable. There is also social proximity, the most important driver for the replication of a model of behaviour, especially if it is virtuous.

As previously discussed, the most important, although most complex, aspect of sustainability choices should be considered. In addition to individual strategies, the firm that is distinguished by a green agenda, inclusive choices and the promotion of employee well-being can have a more powerful impact. At this point we return to a topic discussed above. Bringing about a shift in social priorities and preferences to the point of adopting a more radical set of values that guides a community can seem like an impossible task. Yet, among the most common expressions of Corporate Social Responsibility, there are increasingly frequent actions of territorial education relating to practices that are taken for granted within the firm. It is not uncommon for enterprises to seek to raise awareness in the surrounding communities about safety culture, the green agenda and inclusiveness. One major challenge is determining how business values translate into territorial values. Without doubt, the territory is the ideal platform for assessing the strength of this challenge.

2.4.3 The role of multi-agents for territorial sustainability: The systemic approach

The systemic approach decentralizes the role of firms into a network of multiple entities working together to achieve sustainability goals. It is not necessary to treat the roles as if they were all equal, but rather to consider them all necessary because the various contributions, both in nature and importance, make sustainability strategies feasible at a practical level. The first step is to provide a theoretical foundation for such shared action that emphasizes interaction rather than the strength of the individual agent in shaping the behaviours of others. In addition, this theoretical foundation justifies territorial interaction by leveraging the distinct capabilities of a network of subjects that belong to the territory and are close for reasons of proximity.

The perspective of vital systems provides a theoretical framework for understanding the role of networks and interactions between multiple subjects at the territorial level as a source of sustainability (Simone et al., 2018). According to this perspective, the territory is interpreted as a vital system that is able to survive because the interaction between territorial subjects creates value for all (not only the firm but also public bodies, communities, investors, the natural environment, future generations). Interactions between subjects play an important role in the dissemination of knowledge required for sustainability. Positive interactions are primarily translated into holistic practices, as a result of which the collective outcome is more than just the sum of the individual contributions, but a virtuous multiplier that brings additional value to the collective contributions (Formisano et al., 2018).

Although this approach requires a public actor to play a regulatory role, it does not define the network as an instrument of hierarchical governance, with the public authorities adopting a top-down approach. The vital system employs separate systems collaborating to achieve coordinated results, with the ability to access and share resources by way of coordination mechanisms. Each agent operates within its own network of relationships, acting as a subsystem within the larger territorial system, replicating the same dynamics. In terms of sustainability, the contribution of each agent is the output of its own subsystem in a chain of relationships linking the contributions of each agent. Thus, the public authority is involved in sustainability processes by making a contribution consisting of investigation, definition and decision-making procedures within its own sub-system (Golinelli & Bassano, 2012). Arguably, sustainability is the result of strategic choices that define the possible trajectories of sustainable development based on the decision maker's ability to interpret the context and correctly apply the system of laws. The firm will make a contribution, most likely a sustainability action that is the result of a subsystem of its own economic relations, and so on. A new and more effective point of view emerges, with a broader and stronger solution combining systems of systems, resulting in a complex sustainability strategy generating added value for all the actors contributing to its definition.

The use of the Viable Systems Approach (VSA) as a governance mechanism enables attention to be shifted away from the parties towards the whole. The concept of sustainability becomes especially relevant in the VSA perspective, orienting us towards a broader vision that considers the perspectives of the various stakeholders. This creates a typically recursive bond in which the sustainable choices of the subjects involved increase their chances of survival through the survival of the sub-context in which they operate, and recursively, the survival of higher-level contexts (Golinelli, 2013). Thus, sustainability is the process activated by the components of vital systems as part of a larger system: a process, a dynamic that changes in response to the changing needs of the context and the actors involved. These needs will be social, economic and environmental in nature, requiring differentiated action on the part of all actors involved. The ultimate goal is survival within a territorial configuration that is difficult to replicate in other territories. The distinctive characteristics of sustainability are territorial differences affecting the definition of sustainability objectives. The presence and use of natural resources, human capital, environmental aspects and income distribution have an impact on network actors and system priorities. The two traditional objectives of sustainability, that is, ensuring a sufficient level of quality of life for the population of a territory and achieving sustainable development in a perspective of growth, give rise to the need for an approach that considers the distinctive characteristics of the territory and the actors involved in the accomplishment of sustainability.

The participation that is contingent on the characteristics of the territory is crucial, in the sense that participants must create and interact together in order to generate innovative responses based on their multidisciplinary skills and competencies.

In essence, the firm plays a key role in sustainability, according to this approach. Some process changes may represent technological knowledge that generates social well-being, while also improving the know-how of other firms. However, it is also the case that, in addition to the firm, the synergistic collaboration of other actors and components is required, such as connections, an institutional environment resulting from interaction, a unifying concept of sustainability for the territory and an exchange of information, skills and culture.

2.4.4 Case studies

2.4.4.1 Case study no. 1: The case of the Palestinian women's cooperative

The example of Al-rozana and Al-Thimar, two Palestinian food distribution companies, demonstrates that sustainability is not the exclusive concern of industrialized countries, but that it can function effectively in territories even in conditions of extreme poverty and institutional instability. The work of the two distribution chains is undeniably supported by the international One-Stop-Shop for Sustainable Business Joint Programme, but the initiative of the firm has gone far beyond the expected results of the programme. The initial goal was to promote economic growth and social justice by establishing a network between the distribution chain and rural Palestinian women's cooperatives. However, the positive effects of this project have spread further, increasing the number of actors and initiatives in Palestinian territory and thus shifting the actions of sustainability from an economic to a social transformation. Al-Rozana and Al-Thimar consider Palestinian women's micro-enterprises and cooperatives as a means of facilitating access to markets, which is often difficult, if not impossible, due to the cultural and economic isolation in which women work in Palestine, where they are considered marginal, occasional and thus limited to niche spaces. This was a simple technical support that resulted in two outcomes. The first is economic: the 23 cooperatives managed by women have allowed the two distribution companies to increase their turnover by an average of 40%, providing cooperative products for domestic and international markets. This demonstrates that efficient collaboration among firms increases profits for all the agents involved. However, there is more.

The strong evidence of the women's supply chain has prompted Palestinian public institutions to reconsider their gender policies, including incentives for female entrepreneurship and improved credit access for women's cooperatives. More importantly, the Palestinian regulatory agenda included a recognition of a series of rights and protections for work that had previously been completely disregarded. Significant market protection measures have been implemented in favour of traditional agricultural and cultural products manufactured by women in small- and medium-sized enterprises and cooperatives. In a virtuous cycle, the two distribution chains continue to provide access to local markets for women's cooperatives in the West Bank, while receiving additional support from public institutions and private banks to connect small local businesses to consumer markets.

In a nutshell, this is a sustainable experience producing significant social change. As a consequence, the position of women in the labour market is strengthened by means of direct access to markets previously not accessible to the cooperatives. The stability of the cooperatives is significantly strengthened in this manner. The intervention of the institutions confirms that the processes of sustainability become social changes through their standardization, allowing for the legitimization of equal opportunities extending beyond rural employment and, more broadly, to the working conditions of Palestinian women.

2.4.4.2 *Case study no. 2: Sustainable territorial networks: The Tropical Forest Alliance*

The Tropical Forest Alliance is a multilateral partnership established to support the implementation of actions in the private sector to eliminate deforestation from palm oil, beef, soya and pulp/paper supply chains. Deforestation is primarily associated with raw material production (mainly beef cattle and mining). The network includes approximately 170 partners from companies, government agencies, civil society, indigenous peoples, local communities and international organizations that believe that the challenges posed by the climate emergency cannot be adequately addressed by unilateral or sectoral efforts. This is an essential official initiative to support the process of transitioning supply chains to be deforestation-free. The network focuses on the state of Pará, Brazil's second largest state, which accounts for 9% of the world's tropical forests and has been affected by massive deforestation of over 271,393 km^2, or about 24% of its original area. It is also the most populous state in the Amazon, with approximately 8.6 million residents and a Human Development Index (HDI) of 0.646, compared to Brazil's average HDI of 0.765. (IBGE, 2010). In terms of culture, Pará is one of the most diverse states, with 39 indigenous people. These conditions make it difficult for Pará to begin a process of protecting its rainforest assets alongside sustainable low-carbon socioeconomic development. Pará launched the Tropical Forest Alliance network in 2019 with the aim of transitioning to a more compatible development model that could add value to its socioeconomic resources.

Under the terms of this initiative, support for livestock farming is provided by means of tracking and quotas, allowing for the restoration of pastures or the use of pastures for agriculture, thereby contributing to compliance with the Brazilian Forest Code and the rehabilitation of illegally cleared areas. Simultaneously, the mixed support and control policy is intended to result in a reduction in tropical forest land use, lowering greenhouse gas emissions and improving short-term socioeconomic indicators (BGE 2000–2020). Furthermore, farmers who fail to comply but choose to violate environmental constraints face a number of trade restrictions and are thus excluded from supply chains. The work of the platform has resulted in a number of initiatives, such as the livestock farming code of conduct and the green grains protocol, which are examples of successful partnerships involving the private sector, civil society and state institutions working to reduce deforestation. The intention of the network is to put together policies to encourage environmental, land and production compliance with the goal of slowing deforestation. During the transition period, farmers receive significant assistance ranging from assisted planning to farm management; the provision of free support tools and credit and a credit line developed by the state bank BanPará for farmers who join the programme in exchange for the implementation of their environmental commitments. The network as a whole is intended to be a tool giving socioeconomic impetus to the regions most affected by deforestation, providing an alternative to unsustainable economic models that increase greenhouse gas emissions. In addition to the control and disincentive actions to achieve immediate results in the reduction of deforestation, the programme has a more ambitious long-term goal of bringing about a socio-cultural transformation that is accepted and naturally implemented by all partners. This cultural shift is intended to place the people responsible for deforestation on the front line of long-term environmental protection while supporting economic and production processes, thus representing a significant example of a sustainability programme with the participation of multiple actors.

3 Negative implications of the relationship between the firm and the territory

3.1 Preliminary remarks

This section examines a dimension that is rarely explored, with a view to casting light on illegal practices by firms at a territorial level. The subsections are divided up according to the micro and meso levels to deal with specific questions. In each case, the organizational and theoretical frameworks are considered, as shown in Table 3.1.

3.1.1 The territorial nature of offences committed by firms

This section deals with an issue relating to firms that is not widely explored in organizational studies, especially those focusing on the relationship between the firm and the territory. There is a widespread assumption that this type of analysis is particularly relevant when examining the positive nature of relationships and their impact. The fact that the firm is rooted in the territory is important in terms of the added value both for the firm and the territory. This is a theoretical issue with implications for identity, resilience and sustainability. In most studies, the debate revolves around the implications of positive behaviour on the part of the firm. However, it is possible to approach the issue from another angle, in the sense that the intricate connections between the firm and the territory can favour illegal practices of various kinds.

In line with the concepts examined at the beginning of this study, a territory consists of a network of relationships that benefit from different types of proximity reflecting the distinctive features of the territory. Such relationships can favour fraudulent and illegal practices, due to the relations of proximity. The concept of firms being rooted in the territory is examined here from a different perspective in the sense that shared values and stable relationships resulting from certain unwritten rules can give rise to criminal behaviour. As a result, it is possible to talk about illegal codes of conduct, a culture of illegality, and complicity in the normalization of behaviour harming rather than producing benefits for the community as a whole.

The logical sequence is the same as that which characterizes the positive behaviour of firms with a positive impact on the territory. Firms may use

DOI: 10.4324/9781003365075-4

Table 3.1 Territorial natures of offences committed by firms in two organizational frameworks

Topics	*Territorial nature of the offences committed by a single firm*	*Territorial nature of the offences committed by firms*
Key questions	Why are criminal offences favoured by the relationship between the firm and the territory?	Why do some criminal offences spread across territories?
Theoretical framework	Transaction cost theory	Isomorphism theory
Organizational dimension	Culture/power and structure	Culture
Nature of relationship	Unidirectional	Bidirectional
Level	Micro	Meso

their resources, culture and power to cultivate territorial relations either for legal or illegal purposes.

These relationships need to be examined in a theoretical framework. This is the rationale for explaining the circumstances in which a firm deploys its resources to cultivate relations with the territory even for the purpose of achieving outcomes that are deleterious to the community as a whole. To understand the territorial nature of criminal networks, among the institutional theories, the main insights are drawn from transaction cost theory at the micro level (Williamson, 1996) and organizational isomorphism theory at the meso level (DiMaggio & Powell, 1983). At the micro level, the focus is on the firm as the main actor in order to understand why the criminal contacts that the firm cultivates are supported by its territorial nature. At the meso level, with a focus on the firm as an agent acting among a number of territorial agents, it is possible to cast light on the territorial nature of the firm is likely to result in the spread of illegal activities by a process of imitation.

3.1.1.1 The micro level: Transaction cost theory and the territorial dimension of criminal behaviour

This theoretical approach relies on three key concepts to explain the territorial relationships of firms engaging in criminal behaviour, taking as the starting point the assumption that the main goal of firms is to minimize costs.

Every transaction has specific transaction costs arising from the risk of detection and enforcement. These costs are primarily related to the risks associated with illegal relationships. First of all, detection costs are related to the risk that third parties, either public officials or private firms, will discover the agreement (Lambsdorff & Teksoz, 2004). In contrast, the costs related to enforcement are associated with the risk of poor performance or failure to provide the agreed service (Bowles et al., 2000). Unlike legal transactions, illegal transactions do not offer any legal protection in the event of failure to comply with the terms of the agreement. The cost of enforcement also carries the risk that one of the parties will betray the transaction by reporting it to the authorities.

In addition, these costs reflect the specific properties of the transaction. In particular, three properties are essential to characterize a relationship: the uncertainty that characterizes the relationship, its frequency and asset specificity (Williamson, 2008). The effect of these properties in a transaction gives rise to an increase or reduction in transaction costs. The first property of a transaction is uncertainty, which may be divided into two subcategories: environment and behavioural. Environmental uncertainty concerns unforeseen changes in the environment in which the transaction takes place. A low level of institutional uncertainty indicates the presence of stable and effective institutions in the territory where the transaction takes place (Barasa, 2018).

The efficiency of law enforcement and judicial authorities is widely recognized as a major obstacle to corruption between firms and local authorities. The lower the level of institutional uncertainty, the greater the risk of detection, prosecution and conviction (Troisi et al., 2021; Troisi & Alfano, 2022a). As a secondary risk arising from the transaction, one of the parties could have an incentive to betray the agreement, turning state's evidence in exchange for immunity from prosecution or more lenient treatment.

In contrast, an unstable environment accompanied by a thriving underground economy, with various types of illegal activity, favours illegal transactions by lowering transaction costs, particularly detection costs, because the high volume of criminal activity slows down investigative and judicial actions. Enforcement costs can also be reduced. In this regard, some studies emphasize the fact that a culture of illegality can strengthen the system of threats and punishment in the event of refusing to comply with the conditions laid down in the agreement (Della Porta & Vannucci, 2016). Behavioural uncertainty is a matter of the inability to predict how others will behave. In the case of illegal transactions, the fact that they are not put down in writing and can only be enforced by violence may lead the parties to fail to comply with the agreement (van Winden & Ash, 2012). Behavioural uncertainty significantly increases enforcement and detection costs.

Long-standing relationships, or connections characterized by frequent contacts, reduce enforcement costs while at the same time increasing detection costs. Thanks to ongoing relationships, the parties obtain all sorts of information about the other party, reducing management costs (Basu, 2014). In addition, long-term illegal transactions work more effectively as the threat becomes more credible over time and the rewards become clearer as the parties become more knowledgeable about each other (Lambsdorff & Teksoz, 2004). However, when relationships are long-standing, they tend to be more important than occasional relationships.

Asset specificity is related to the extent to which an asset applies only to a particular transaction. If the transaction is not successfully implemented, the asset cannot be easily reassigned to another transaction without significant loss of the value of the investment. (Williamson, 1996). Real estate investments, physical assets and human capital tend to be specific to a particular transaction. The degree of specificity of the asset invested in a particular transaction increases the risk of opportunism and thus enforcement costs (Barasa, 2018). In the case of tangible assets, the assets can be easily traced and verification costs tend to be high.

This leads on to our next point: the parties seek to mitigate the costs arising from the transaction in order to maximize the benefits from the transaction. The argument put forward here is that the territory is a means for reducing costs. Since it brings together three types of proximity, it serves to reduce the risks relating to illegal transactions, thus allowing actors to benefit from territorial relations. In essence, an illegal transaction that takes place in a specific territory tends to be less risky than a transaction between a firm and an agent not belonging to the same territory.

Social proximity can also mitigate enforcement costs. Due to the relationship of trust and long-term bonds, the parties can reduce the risk of a breach of contract. Geographical and technological proximity reduce detection costs by allowing transactions to be implemented between actors with the same level of know-how. This can activate a set of mechanisms to disguise illegal transactions (Troisi & Alfano, 2022b). The territorial dimension of an illegal transaction can result in the same benefits as a legal transaction. Transaction cost theory casts light on how the territory can function as a useful context in both cases.

3.1.1.2 The meso level: The neo-institutional theory of isomorphism

When a number of agents operate in the same organizational field, intended here as a territory, they tend to imitate each other. DiMaggio and Powell (1983) framed this process as isomorphic pressure. Rather than increasing efficiency, the adoption of standard patterns of behaviour tends to strengthen the legitimacy of firms and their actions. Isomorphic theory distinguishes between the following three types of imitation:

- *Coercive isomorphism*: This refers to the pressure exerted by institutions in complementary ways at different levels. Institutional pressure leads to similar behaviour on the part of firms, the frequency of which depends on the degree of institutional pressure.
- *Mimetic isomorphism*: In this case, in an environment of uncertainty and limited rationality, firms tend to imitate one another, replicating practices by means of a domino effect following the agents who have

greater credibility or are considered leaders in a particular organizational field.

- *Regulatory isomorphism*: This is a dynamic that underpins the professionalization of the members of an organizational field, through professional networks. However, it is cited here for theoretical reasons, not because it is relevant for the purposes of the present study.

Isomorphism has been extensively studied with particular reference to the best practices it produces but only a few studies consider the negative aspects of imitation (Venard, 2009; Troisi & Alfano, 2022b, Chen et al., 2018). In fact, conditions in favour of imitative behaviour can help propagate both legal and illegal practices. Isomorphism tends to favour the replication of actions, leading either to positive or negative outcomes. As a result, two propositions can be put forward. First, since imitation is a neutral term, there may be negative effects arising from imitative practices. Second, the territory appears to be a powerful vector of imitation. In terms of coercive isomorphism, institutions exert pressure on agents' behaviour in various ways. This is because at local level, all agents are subject to the same pressure as they operate in the same area. In essence, a low level of institutional pressure gives rise to non-compliance of a similar level, given that there is some level of regulation and enforcement with a local impact that is the responsibility of the territorial institutions.

Similar considerations apply to mimetic isomorphism. When a firm engages in illegal or improper market practices, and these practices are useful to other firms or agents as the costs of illegal behaviour are lower than the benefits, the agents who are geographically closest are likely to imitate this behaviour. They will be aware of the illegal practices due to geographic proximity (by way of example, cases of illegal land use or building without planning permission may well be visible from neighbouring properties), or because they are located in the same district, they have the same know-how, and tend to imitate this behaviour to reduce costs and gain market advantages.

The negative effects of the relationship with the territory are explored further in the following, distinguishing between the micro level and the meso level.

3.2 Why crimes committed by firms tend to be territorial

At this point, it is important to examine in depth the reasons why criminal behaviour is favoured by the relationship with the territory at micro level. In the framework of transaction cost theory, we examine all three organizational dimensions.

Transaction cost theory can help explain in greater depth why firms tend to commit crimes that are predominantly rooted in the territory. We can distinguish between asset specificity and the other properties of the transaction since they refer to two conditions in which the firm employs different strategies for reducing transaction costs. They are related to various territorial factors that lead firms to commit crimes intrinsically linked to the territory as a strategy to reduce transaction costs.

Asset specificity may serve as a useful starting point. Specific types of asset are typical of the firm's relationship with the territory, in connection with both positive and negative outcomes (Barasa, 2018).

The territory where an organization operates can give rise to dependency in terms of both tangible and intangible resources. Firms require raw materials, employees, capital, reputation management and personal obligations (Gaur et al., 2015). At the same time, the regulatory authorities in a given territory can give rise to many issues for firms, and may be a source of dependency as public institutions grant rights and status (Greenwood & Tao, 2021).

This question is primarily a matter of power in the micro-organizational dimension. The greater the dependency of the firm on territorial resources, the greater the imbalance of power in favour of the owner of the resources. When a particular asset is utilized for a transaction, the concepts of resource dependency and power asymmetry become relevant for transaction cost theory. The firm purchases labour from the territory that makes available its specific human capital. In addition, the firm procures raw materials from the territory, and pays for public services such as waste disposal that are provided on a monopolistic basis. In all these cases, alternative resources are not as readily available in geographical terms as the local resources, so unless the firm identifies readily available resources incurring additional transport costs, the territorial resources cannot be replaced.

Agents outside the firm can raise the price of their services until they reach the highest price the firm is prepared pay to reduce its dependence on local resources. If prices remain below this threshold, these territorial agents obtain a return on investment deriving from the specific asset.

These actors play a central role in these relationships and thus determine their dynamics. Essentially, geographical proximity can give rise to dependence for the firm since suppliers, workers, banks and local institutions, whether private or public, are largely territorial. Arguably, the greater the firm's reliance on territorial resources, the more likely it is that the firm will engage in criminal behaviour.

According to resource dependence theory, firms seek to reduce the uncertainty associated with dependence when environmental conditions are not sufficient to readily obtain resources (Hillman et al., 2009). One possible strategy to reduce dependency, and mitigate the costs relating to the specific investment is to procure similar resources by means of self-processing or outsourcing. In this way, firms manage to operate without external resources by providing resources themselves or by outsourcing tasks to other suppliers (Drees & Heugens, 2013). A policy of this kind may require illegal access to resources. Although this is commonly regarded as a standard break-up strategy (Cuervo-Cazurra, 2016), the methods adopted by firms for reducing dependency vary. The severity of the crime committed by the firm determines the nature of the break-up strategy.

The logical sequence is as follows. The firm depends on territorial resources, and these territorial resources require specific investments. When the owners of resources raise their prices, the power asymmetry becomes excessive, allowing firms to terminate relationships and make up for the lack of legal resources with illegal resources. This is a low-cost strategy in monetary terms, but much more dangerous. A specific case may be used to clarify this concept. If the public authority or contractor increases the cost of waste disposal, the service is the only one in the territory, provided on an exclusive basis, and forcing the firm to continue to use this provider for a period of time. However, if the cost is too high, the firm may be encouraged to engage in illegal practices to manage the disposal of industrial waste. The monetary cost of illegal services tends to be low. Clearly, no administrative costs are incurred in illegal waste disposal, and as a result, low prices can be set to encourage businesses to use this type of service. The real cost of illegal waste disposal is the risk of detection since it can result in prosecution and reputational damage. But once again, geographical proximity plays a role in this case. The risk of detection is mitigated by the proximity of the agents, resulting in shorter delivery times and, as a result, a reduced risk of detection for the agents engaging in the illegal transaction.

Although labour costs are determined by national agreement or by law, territorial resources tend to exhibit a degree of specialization, making them specific resources with added value in the transaction. If the cost of these resources increases, the firm can be encouraged to use undeclared labour, reducing costs and paying cash-in-hand for the services provided. Taken to the extreme, this leads to the system of illegal gangmasters, a system known in Italy as *caporalato*, in which agricultural firms hire non-EU workers, often undocumented immigrants, who are paid under the table, often a pitiful sum that bears no relation to the hours worked in the fields (Reyneri, 1998; Maddaloni & Moffa, 2021). As in other sectors of the informal economy, firms tend to replace the local labour force with immigrant workers, often undocumented workers, who are not covered by health and insurance contributions or any other employment protection measures.

Numerous examples of illegal practices may be cited, and the specific investment may represent an excessive burden for the firm depending on the circumstances. As a result, it can adopt a counter-balancing strategy by turning an asymmetric position to its advantage, or at the very least by entering into a new relationship in which it finds itself in a less disadvantageous asymmetric position than the previous one. Consider credit facilities from local banks. When the credit facility is deemed to be too expensive or no longer available, the firm may resort to usury. In this case, the firm is likely to obtain a loan at a higher cost, resulting in an imbalance of power but lowering the cost of access to credit at least initially.

In each of these situations, the degree of seriousness of the crime committed is closely related to the level of resource dependency (Jiang et al., 2021). It may be assumed that in cases in which the resource dependency is perceived by the firm to be burdensome, the severity of the crime committed as a way to address the problem is likely to increase. With reference to our example, this means greater recourse to the dumping of industrial waste, the employment of undocumented labour with the workers paid cash-in-hand, and recourse to usury.

In all these situations, the mitigation of the costs arising from the specific investment is intended to counterbalance an asymmetric relationship. The parties are in an exchange relationship and in conflict in terms of power. In some cases, the parties cooperate in the crime and benefit from social and technical proximity to mitigate the costs arising from behavioural and environmental uncertainty (Troisi & Alfano, 2022b). Some examples may be cited to illustrate this point. Many studies show that corruption, considered the most important economic crime committed by firms, is rarely committed selectively or in isolation (Ibodullaevich & Bahromovna, 2020; Cuervo-Cazurra, 2016; Venard, 2009). On the contrary, it is a recurring act within an integrated network. This is a valid assumption for both public and private corruption. In both cases, the pattern of committing the offence presents the same characteristics. Corrupt agreements involving several firms, or firms and public officials, are the outcome of a territorial network characterized by customary practices that reflect a tacit agreement to break the law. There are two main organizational aspects to consider here: the structure that enables the firm to systematically expand its activities across a network, and the cultural aspect (Lambsdorff & Teksoz, 2004).

Collusive agreements within a territorial network can mitigate the costs of the corrupt relationship. The frequency of transactions reduces the risk of betrayal, while increasing the chances that the corrupt deal will be implemented as agreed. Social and technological proximity play a key role here. The proximity of the parties increases the likelihood of the transaction being implemented in compliance with the terms negotiated by the parties. The closer the parties, and the more they share the same know-how, the greater the incentive to conclude corrupt deals. They possess the appropriate expertise to prevent their criminal actions being detected, enabling them to stay "under the radar". In addition, the bond of trust that binds the parties together can encourage the replication of criminal acts over time. In what they consider to be a "virtuous circle", the closer the parties from a social and cultural point of view, the more the transactions tend to be replicated over time. Conversely, the closer the relationship over time, the closer the parties from a social point of view. In addition, proximity reduces the cost of behavioural uncertainty. A learning process takes place, upgrading the skills required for fraudulent deals and improving the knowledge of the other parties involved. Any uncertainty resulting from opportunistic behaviour is avoided, at least partially, by enhancing the knowledge of the technological capabilities of the other party, and ensuring the necessary level of trust (Troisi & Alfano, 2022b).

Like most cases of fraud, corruption tends to be territorial by nature. In particular, the corruption of public officials is a means of resolving the problem of reliance on public resources. This includes the payment of bribes for the award of public contracts or reducing the time required to obtain permits or planning permission. However, public officials who take bribes in exchange for providing public services are not unknown agents with whom the firms attempt to initiate a corrupt relationship. They are typically agents with personal contact and close links to firms, and as a result the corrupt practices are characterized by frequency and trust (Della Porta & Vannucci, 2016). These criminal actions depend on social proximity and are intended to reduce costs, though, as noted above, they carry the risk that one of the parties will fail to implement the agreement or even report it to the judicial authorities.

Cases in which firms commit crimes with a high level of environmental uncertainty are also characterized by territorial characteristics. Local culture and business practice tend to move in the same direction. As a result, in many cases firms are located in territories where lack of respect for the rule of law in its various forms is tolerated and normalized. There is a link between the illegal behaviour of the firm and the practices allowed or widely tolerated in the territory. If the firm fails to comply with the law, this does not necessarily result in reputational damage as it reflects the local environment, characterized by a particular set of values. Territories in which criminal organizations are active are those in which a culture of illegality has an impact on many other agents, not just on the criminal organization strictly speaking.

In Italy, the official data (Istat, 2020) show that the territories where Mafia-type organizations operate are those with high levels of undocumented labour, environmental crimes and corruption of both public officials and private-sector managers. Some businesses, even those not forming part of traditional criminal networks, adopt the same logic. They are legally incorporated, but engage in illegal practices along the lines of criminal organizations.

These practices may be interpreted according to transaction cost theory, along with the discussion of proximity. Firm that engage in illegal practices in an uncertain environment may be encouraged to do so because the risk of enforcement and detection is low. From the point of view of enforcement, a territory with a prevalent culture of illegality has its own codes of conduct according to which it is not permitted to betray the agreement, or where the likelihood of betrayal is low, given that the risk of punitive action is evident. At the same time, detection costs are low because committing offences in a criminal environment with high rates of illegal behaviour reduces the risk of detection. Proximity allows for one further consideration. Territories characterized by high levels of social proximity, while unusual, are places where criminal activity is widely tolerated as normal. Social disapproval is practically

Table 3.2 Properties of transactions, role of proximity and territorial implications

	Territorial proximity			
	Technological proximity	*Social proximity*	*Geographical proximity*	*Territorial implications*
Assets specificity			x	Unlawful acts to break dependency.
Frequency of transaction		x	x	A criminal agreement with several occurrences throughout time.
Environmental uncertainty		x	x	Enhancement of illegality's territorial culture.
Behavioural uncertainty	x		x	Confidence in committing a joint unlawful acts.

non-existent, and firm contribute to reinforcing the view that the territory is beyond the bounds of legality. Table 3.2 summarizes the effects of transaction properties at the territorial level, as well as the role of proximity.

3.3 Why some forms of criminal behaviour become widespread across territories

At meso level, it is well known that in certain territories illegal behavior is based on imitation, spreading from one firm to another. This is mainly due to weak territorial institutions, along with the prevailing culture of illegality (Banerjee, 2019). Two examples from Italy may be cited to highlight the territorial nature of corruption and the spread of illegal land use by firms on a territorial basis propagated by a process of imitation.

Firms tend to imitate each other for a number of reasons. The common denominator of imitation derives from the legitimacy that a certain form of behaviour can acquire rather than the actual advantage to be obtained. The literature on isomorphic behaviour is primarily concerned with the study of imitative practices, governance or structural choices with a positive impact, as a result of which the firm is highly regarded (Wei et al., 2017). Isomorphic behaviour is explained by a sort of domino effect. It is supported by the idea of conforming to the choices made by the majority of firms rather than purely rational criteria. This applies to actions, decisions and business strategies. When firms imitate each other in a negative way, the situation is fundamentally different. If firms fail to comply with the law, others may follow suit. In this case, the reasons for the legitimacy cannot justify these choices, because in the case of illegal practices there is no official recognition by the market. On the contrary, if firms imitate each other mainly by engaging in illegal practices, the aim is a reduction in costs. Therefore, the practices are illegal but deemed to be absolutely rational in terms of maximizing profits (Venard, 2009). Consider, by way of example, the imitative dynamics of the corruption of public officials: firms can conclude a corrupt agreement with a public official because the payment of a bribe can be considered to be the price to circumvent the legal procedures required to obtain a benefit such as a licence or, more broadly, the right to carry out a procedure necessary for the operation of the business. In either case, the firm aims to reduce costs by obtaining the necessary permits without following normal procedures, thus eliminating concealed risks.

Another example could be the process for obtaining planning permission. Even more evident is the corruption of public officials by firms in connection with tenders, with the payment of bribes to ensure that the firm is awarded the contract during the bidding process. In cases of criminal behaviour, the firm cannot acquire legitimacy by a process of imitation. A logic of cost saving can give rise to a range of different actions. Specifically, decision-making by a firm intending to mimic the non-compliant behaviour of another firm may be explained as follows. Cost is an important consideration for any firm, and cost-saving enables the firm to survive. Under certain conditions, if savings are illegal and there is a low risk of being prosecuted and sentenced for such conduct, a firm may be encouraged to commit an offence once other firms have done so.

In addition, the fact that such illegal practices have already taken place and are widespread among firms shows that they are considered to be widely acceptable, making it easier to replicate them. The more firms engage in criminal activity, the more the culture of illegality is reinforced. As a result, firms can be confident of a low risk of detection and sanctions, and even less risk of reputational damage.

This assumption is necessary to examine in greater depth the process of imitation on the part of firms. It is necessary to understand why illegal practices become widespread at the territorial level by means of a process of imitation, and as we shall see, a particular type of imitation.

Studies on isomorphism highlight the factors justifying the dissemination of specific practices, driven by imitative behaviour between firms, and identify them in relation to external pressures. As mentioned above, the concepts of coercive isomorphism and mimetic isomorphism, and the associated pressures, are deemed to be particularly useful for the purposes of this study. Pressures giving rise to imitative behaviour are the same as those that shape positive practices. Arguably, the same kind of pressure can be used to lead to negative practices, and is particularly significant when firms are located in the same territory. To return to an earlier point, the territory functions as an organizational field in which agents influenced by the same institutional logic resemble each other for a variety of reasons. To begin with, firms tend to replicate the same types of behaviour because they are influenced by the same institutional pressure (Koroso et al., 2019).

There is substantial empirical evidence in the literature, particularly in the economic literature, for the claim that strong institutions provide a positive guide for the behaviour of communities, including firms (Niyobuhungiro & Schenck, 2021). On the contrary, weak and ineffective institutions tend to encourage rule-breaking behaviour (Lian et al., 2019).

This assumption is particularly significant at the local level. Territorial institutions play an important role in a narrow field of action that is more focused on the needs of local communities. As a result, both their strengths and weaknesses are immediately apparent. This leads on to the following questions: What are the territorial institutions that can put pressure on firms? What is meant by the strength or weakness of an institution? How do they direct imitational behaviour?

As noted above, territorial institutions may be classified as formal or informal. Both help to define the institutional logic of the organizational field, which can be examined by identifying a territorial area for the sake of simplicity.

Regulatory institutions are among the local territorial institutions with an immediate capacity to govern the behaviour of firms. Regulatory institutions at the local level, in accordance with the provisions at national level, aim at regulating the economic or civil life of a specific community within a given territory (Koroso et al., 2019).

The rules vary from country to country, but the general principles in many states assign important powers to the local level, and the powers at territorial level enable institutions to regulate various aspects of economic life. For example, many local authorities recognize the right to set up community-based businesses. Regulations vary from place to place, but they all work according to a territorial plan. Territorial-level governance is usually a combination of regulations that lay down rights and obligations, establish rules and determine administrative procedures. At the territorial level, the authorities play both regulatory and administrative roles, both of which affect the territory. For example, municipalities in many countries combine regulatory and administrative functions. The regulations that have the greatest impact on the economic life of a community include planning functions, both urban and rural, with the ability to determine the rules governing a firm's behaviour at local level.

In addition to administrative and regulatory bodies, there are bodies dedicated to enforcement at territorial level. The local police, judiciary, environmental protection authorities and labour inspectorate responsible for monitoring violations of local regulations are all granted local jurisdiction (Dur & Vollaard, 2019). Clearly, the judicial authority, which is a national institution, exercises its function at the territorial level and deals with cases relating to the territory in accordance with the rules of the national jurisdiction.

Finally, local political institutions often cultivate close relations with top management at the territorial level, either through overlapping responsibilities, or at least with a certain degree of continuity of roles. Local governments, judicial and political institutions are characterized by a degree of interdependence that is difficult to identify at other levels (Troisi & Alfano, 2022a). In this connection, the reasons for supporting strong or weak institutions across the territory affect all local institutions at the same time due to strong networks. Consequently, institutional weaknesses affect the related institutions. Let us take an example: significant political instability, with a rapid turnover of mayors, and the appointment of special administrators due to insolvency or other reasons affecting the stability of the institutions, all have immediate effects on territorial governance. The lack of certainty at the political level reflects the difficulties in the administration due to factors of contiguity. If political strategies are lacking, it is difficult to imagine efficient governance at local level, and law enforcement that works without a clear definition of the behaviour expected of the community.

The judiciary plays a different role. Even if its authority is confined within administrative boundaries, it deals with nationally important issues. However, it is undeniable that it can be drawn into the local network consisting of a number of different agencies. There is another issue that needs to be investigated, which is a key characteristic of institutions at the local level. Institutional strengths or weaknesses are an attribute that depends on both the community and the institution. One measure of institutional efficiency is how well an institution governs the behaviour of the local community. Clearly, there is no way to govern behaviour effectively unless it is accepted by the community. Although institutions can work well formally speaking, there is essentially a gap between the role of the institution and the needs of the community. Such a gap can have immediate implications at local level. It relates to the specific interests of a particular community and is immediately recognized as such. Consequently, powerful institutions need to be efficient and accepted by the local community (Koroso et al., 2019).

At the same time, weak institutions are inefficient and lack legitimacy. All local agencies contribute to a climate of general trust, or the opposite, a climate of distrust in the institutions. When institutions are perceived to be ineffective or lacking in legitimacy, they tend to bring other institutions down with them. In our case, the weakness of regulatory bodies tends to give rise to a lack of trust in officials in general. If the system is perceived as weak and there is a climate of distrust, the community tends to behave in two ways. First, it can refuse to support the institutional framework, no longer relying on political incentives, legal remedies or general public support. In such cases, the community shows scant regard for weak institutions and acts independently. Next, and this is an interesting phenomenon at the heart of the discussion, in the presence of weak institutions, the members of the community that are in direct contact with these institutions act in violation of the rules (Chen et al., 2018). For example, administrative rules that require the payment of excessive local taxes may lead to violations. Firms and individuals may choose not to pay for public services, not to comply with the restrictions on concessions, and not to respect the terms and conditions of the permits granted. This tends to reduce administrative costs, but in particular shows a lack of awareness on the part of regulatory bodies, and at the same time a deterrent effect in relation to enforcement agencies. Firms that pay bribes gain easier access to administrative services. This undermines the effectiveness of regulatory agencies and at the same time undermines the capabilities of the police and judicial authorities.

If this strategy is successful, it becomes customary to replicate such practices, especially if the illegal payment achieves the expected cost savings with a low risk of detection and enforcement. This is the essence of coercive isomorphism. Weak institutions at the local level not only lead to disorientation, but also engender widespread distrust that encourages illicit behaviour. According to related studies on isomorphism, if these practices are associated with corporate crime at territorial level, there are two further outcomes. First, they have a greater impact in terms of the total area of the territory affected in relation to larger geographical areas such as regions or the nation (Niyobuhungiro & Schenck, 2021; Tang et al., 2021).

The local area is essentially a hotspot for the epidemic of corporate crime. Second, there is a related link between the weakness of the local system and the seriousness of the crimes committed. The weaker the local system is perceived to be, the greater the incidence of crime, both in frequency and severity. The final argument depends strictly on the territorial nature of the isomorphism. On the one hand, it is a strong reaction to institutions close to the firm, and on the other, the possibility of witnessing the impunity of other firms due to geographical proximity, stimulates negative behaviour and increases the level of seriousness (Ufere et al., 2020). The reason for the increase in severity is easily explained by the nature of negative isomorphism, which, unlike positive isomorphism, results in cost savings rather than enabling the agent to gain legitimacy.

The more serious the crime, the more likely it is that the cost of certain business activities will be reduced. The most serious territorial offences usually result in a slew of negative externalities with a deleterious effect on the community. For example, the repeated illegal disposal of industrial waste increases the seriousness of the crime since it causes significant environmental damage while reducing business costs as the illegal method is preferred over the legal method more than once. Similarly, releasing toxic substances into the environment increases the severity of the offence while reducing the cost of doing business. Firms that imitate each other tend to go from bad to worse, as the risk of being detected or convicted is lower. In short, in the case of coercive isomorphism, the increasing severity is accompanied by tangible cost savings for firms, while the intangible cost in terms of risk is reduced.

Another variety of isomorphism is known as mimetic. This consists of a horizontal form of isomorphism in which a firm adopts certain practices that were previously successfully adopted by other firms (Chen et al., 2018). The role of the institution reappears and is understood here in its informal aspects. Firms tend to imitate market practices, even those that are illegal, that are widespread in their industries or regions. In this sense, they are informal or unwritten rules. They are widely used, presenting a low level of risk, and have been shown to reduce costs, and therefore appear to be viable and effective options for the firm.

This argument is particularly relevant in the case of mimetic isomorphism, where this dynamic is influenced by the concentration of the proximities characterizing the territory. This concentration leads to an escalation of offences of the same severity facilitated by the presence of weak institutions at the local level. But why does mimetic isomorphism particularly benefit from territorial advantages in the case of irregular practices?

Specific geographical proximity, often in the form of technical proximity, plays a role, but social proximity, which connects businesses in particular, is a powerful vector of many imitative mechanisms, especially illegal ones (Singh et al., 2021). Geographical proximity, as in the case of institutional isomorphism, makes it easier for other firms to witness the practices adopted by other firms. The use of buildings for unauthorized purposes, such as when agricultural premises are used for unauthorized events, illegal land use and failure to reduce carbon emissions in the same area are observable by other firms (Calabrò, 2020). Again, by enabling other firms to witness illicit practices, firms show that they are committing an offence with impunity. Unscrupulous firms seeking to maximize profits and reduce costs will tend to imitate (Bologna, 2017). Many firms engage in unethical or illegal behaviour more readily when violations in a given area leave no immediate trace, implying that other firms will enjoy a similar degree of impunity. However, technical proximity is a powerful vector if a firm needs specific techniques to engage in illegal practices.

It may be argued that social proximity represents the most powerful driver of mimetic isomorphism. The culture of illegality that is widespread in a given territory is the most powerful means of replication of tax evasion or violation of other rules and regulations including planning regulations. In many cases, informal rules or unwritten codes of conduct promote illegal practices that are rooted in a particular territory. What is allowed and normalized is the result of previous experience, a set of beliefs and assumptions that reinforce each other and are reproduced within territorial boundaries. In addition, when social proximity is found to be the connective tissue of a territory characterized by a culture of illegality, it is more likely for the imitative behaviour to be of a serious nature.

There are two reasons for this. One is that normalization of criminal activity reinforces the perception that it is harmless and can be replicated. In contrast, in an environment where a culture of illegality is widespread, the number of offences of various kinds increases, and enforcement measures become complicated. In addition, another aspect is worth mentioning, relating to the fact that mimetic isomorphism is a particular territorial issue. It is well known that it depends on conditions of uncertainty in the market in which the firm operates. As a result, the greater the need for rapid change as required by the market, the less robust and responsive the firm is likely to be. In response to market pressures, firms may transform some of their activities into illegal businesses and achieve the cost savings mentioned above (Hanousek et al., 2021. In addition to the pressure due to market uncertainty, sales and supply chains can also exert pressure. Small and medium-sized enterprises typically set up productive facilities within certain territorial boundaries. As these markets shrink, it becomes a problem for the firms that are contiguous in territorial terms. It is often the case that bankruptcies occur frequently in certain territories because access to credit facilities from local banks may be restricted, or raw materials may no longer be available. What is frequently perceived to be solely a characteristic of national markets can actually be a much stronger driving force when it comes to pressure from markets in the territory where the firm operates. Essentially, local businesses are particularly exposed to changes in adjacent markets because they are shared. Market pressure is often seen only in terms of markets at national level. However, territorial market pressure can also be a strong driving force.

In conclusion, when institutional and mimetic pressure is exerted by the territories where firms operate, this results in imitative practices that can escalate in severity over a short period of time (Figure 3.1).

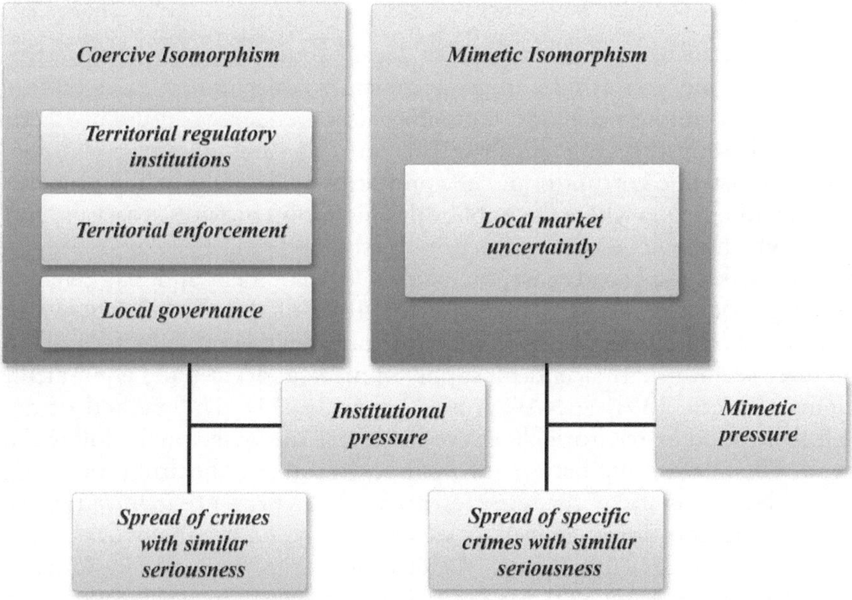

Figure 3.1 The influence of isomorphism on the territorial spread of crimes.

3.4 Case studies

3.4.1 Case study no. 1: The dynamics of territorial corruption

Our analysis of the judgements of the Court of Cassation, Italy's highest criminal court, along with the reports from the national anti-corruption agency, does not provide a complete picture of the level of corruption, but it does cast light on some important features. In this analysis, a total of 360 public judgements were investigated, dealing with cases of corruption involving firms and public officials.

The judgements were taken from the Court of Cassation website (www.italgiure.it) for the period from 2018 to 2022. Two types of corruption are found in the dynamic relationship between firms and public officials. The first consists of isolated cases of corruption. For example, a company may approach public officials to obtain a permit or licence in a timely manner or to obtain preferential treatment in a public tender. This type of corruption is characterized by two major features. The first consists of the fact that the firm is not necessarily local. The public official may be solely responsible for the provision of public services. The cost of corruption to obtain preferential treatment in the provision of public services is generally high. The rationale is to reduce the risk of betrayal in the absence of a relationship of trust, direct control and direct knowledge of the other party, in the absence of any form of proximity. Payment of a bribe is thus an additional price, typically in cash, that the firm pays in the event of an occasional transaction in which the risks are high and thus mitigation requires the payment of a large sum.

These cases of occasional corruption are in contrast with the more frequent, systematic, territorial and geographically concentrated cases of corruption in the southern regions, and, albeit less frequently, in the northern regions following the same pattern. The ratio of cases of occasional corruption to systemic corruption is 1:8, primarily concerning public procurement, including cases where the public administration provides a service, and cases in which the government procures outsourced public services.

Public works in a broad sense, including redevelopment and maintenance (building, road, site security), account for 40% of the total. Next, waste management (collection, transportation, management, landfill; 22%) and the healthcare sector (pharmaceutical, supply of medical devices and equipment, cleaning services; 13%) (ANAC annual report, 2021). The method of defining corruption on territorial lines can be carried out based on the following criteria. The relationship between the public official and the firm is ongoing, and they both operate on the same territory. Other firms are involved in the network of relationships, as well as various public bodies. Networks often contain political elements. Finally, the cost of corruption varies in terms of quantity and type. Along with the other actors, firms adopt specific strategies to negotiate corrupt deals that remain undetected.

Corruption cases can be classified based on the value of the contract: various mechanisms including the construction of cartels between multiple companies are typical particularly of high value contracts. This is reflected in the minimum discount compared to the starting price for bids. However, in the case of low-value transactions, it is common to co-opt lower levels of management by means of an exchange of favours, such as hiring family members from the network rather than the company that is awarded the contract. Offences committed by public officials include the award of contracts without proper selection procedures, the improper use of emergency powers, open bidding with the specification in the tender designed to favour corrupt companies, and multiple bidding procedures from the same provider. Other improper procedures include the extension of expired contracts, especially in the waste management sector, the lack of proper auditing procedures, particularly in the construction of public works, and the award of contracts based on rigged bidding procedures.

Overall, based on the cases examined in the database, corrupt exchanges proceed according to a regulatory mechanism that ensures widespread compliance with informal rules, and in various forms, depending on the dominant role played by the various actors. It becomes clear that they manage to exert power of various kinds (political, administrative and entrepreneurial), all connected in the same territory.

Cash payments appear to be comparatively rare. Cash is still the primary means of payment for illegal agreements, but for small amounts (2,000–3,000 euros, in some cases as little as 50–100 euros) and it may be a percentage of the value of the public contract. The difficulty of hiding sums of money from unspecified or illegal sources leads to new and more flexible forms of corruption, in particular, the promise of hiring spouses, relatives, or individuals who are otherwise involved in the case of corruption.

This is followed by the provision of professional services, particularly consultancy services, to individuals or legal entities associated with the corrupt (or complacent) public official. In rare cases, gifts are provided. The database provides data on the goods and services provided in these cases, more than a fifth of the total, to confirm the multiple forms of corruption (21%). In addition to material benefits (fuel, meals, overnight stays), there are also benefits of other kinds (building renovations, repairs, cleaning services, furniture transport, carpentry work, gardening, painting), and sometimes sexual services. The value of the bribes in some cases is modest, demonstrating the ease with which public services can be traded for personal gain.

Overall, it is clear from the cases that have come to light that corrupt exchanges take place according to stable regulatory mechanisms that ensure widespread compliance with a set of unwritten rules that take on different characteristics depending on the role played by the centres of power (political, bureaucratic and entrepreneurial) all linked to the same territory.

Local businesses engage in transactions with public officials in a network that involves politicians and other agents who benefit from the advantages of proximity in lowering transaction costs. To sum up, they are linked by long-standing, territorial relationships of an illegal kind that entirely displace legal relationships.

3.4.2 Case study no. 2: Isomorphism and illegal land use

The map in Figure 3.2 is intended to cast light on how illegal land use takes place by means of isomorphic dynamics, each with a specific incidence depending on the territory.

Figure 3.2 Map of cases of illegal land use by firms. (Author's elaboration of Court of Cassation judgements and ANAC annual report.)

Firms engaging in illegal land use open the door to a wide range of inappropriate behaviour. Broadly speaking, the land is used inefficiently, primarily for unauthorized purposes. The difference between the various kinds of illegal land use and the degree of severity is calculated as follows. The larger the area affected by illegal land use, the more serious the offence is deemed to be. Regardless of the type of illegal land use, the common denominator is that firms use land on which no construction work is planned for business purposes.

In addition, where illegal land use is related to organized crime, the degree of seriousness of the land use offences taking place in the area tends to be greater than in others, because it typically combines both the calculation of the total area affected, and the violation of areas protected for conservation reasons. In essence, there is an escalation of the gravity of the offence that is associated with low levels of institutional pressure, which is typical of territories where Mafia-type organizations thrive. The fact that cases of a serious nature are tolerated in these areas gives rise to a process of imitation, resulting in an escalation of the environmental consequences.

Conclusions

This chapter offers an overview of the key takeaways of the theoretical analysis and case studies. The theoretical framework outlined is examined to redefine the concept of territorial organization. Future avenues for research are then outlined.

The analysis was intended to offer a fresh perspective on firms and the territories in which they operate. The main findings of the study are as follows.

The first consists of a definition: the territory is a relational space shaped by its history and rooted in the present. It has its own specific characteristics with which the firm must contend, adapting its organizational dimensions for that specific territory, which cannot necessarily be replicated elsewhere.

The second consists of a proposal for a criterion that is rarely used in studies of the firm and the territory. Proximity is a key criterion for defining and interpreting spaces as argued in this study. The manner in which it is presented highlights the distinctive characteristics of territories.

The third consists of insights of the positive and negative implications of the relationship between the firm and the territory.

With regard to the positive implications, three key concepts must be considered.

The first is territorial identity, examined in an institutional perspective, casting light on the fact that firms and their territories can give rise to a virtuous circle in which they mutually influence each other, creating their own rules and endogenous development practices.

The second is the resilience of the firm, which has positive territorial implications closely related to the flexibility of the firm. In addition, territorial resilience, defined as the capacity of a territory to respond to external shocks, frequently places the firm in the position of key actor, intervening rapidly as a result of technological proximity.

The third is the sustainability of the firm, responding to the need to shape organizational factors to promote the well-being of its territory. Like resilience, sustainability of the territory is frequently achieved as a result of the consolidation of the key role of the firm in the territory.

With regard to the negative implications, in general, there is a territorial dimension to corporate crime, in the same way as positive action by firms

DOI: 10.4324/9781003365075-5

can be enhanced territorial roots. When criminal offences are territorial in nature, they benefit from the advantages of network and proximity that are far less common than in the case of non-territorial crimes. The other essential element for casting light on territorial crimes is their replication by means of imitation, which is a powerful phenomenon due to its mimetic force. The severity of the offences tends to increase over time in an escalation resulting from the sharing of territorial institutions that tend to be weak or ineffective in terms of law enforcement.

While not claiming to be exhaustive, the study offers a number of suggestions. The primary intention was to outline a different perspective that could provide an in-depth understanding of the relationship between the firm and the territory, while explaining its underlying rationale. Certain elements bind firms to the territory, and this insight paves the way forward for future research. The firm with strong links to the territory can become a concept in its own right explaining the survival of firms and their characteristics of proximity. The focus needs to be on the firm's strategies, behaviour and territorial characteristics. It is the firm that determines a model that is not necessarily diametrically opposed to that of global enterprise. The in-depth analysis of the dynamics of growth, development and survival is likely to represent a strand of research of great interest for scholars in various disciplines in the years ahead.

References

Aarikka-Stenroos, L., & Ritala, P. (2017). 'Network management in the era of ecosystems: Systematic review and management framework'. *Industrial Marketing Management*, *67*, 23–36.

Abba, M., Yahaya, L., & Suleiman, N. (2018). 'Explored and critique of contingency theory for management accounting research'. *Journal of Accounting and Financial Management ISSN*, *4*(5), 40–50.

Acs, Z. J., Autio, E., & Szerb, L. (2014). 'National systems of entrepreneurship: Measurement issues and policy implications'. *Research Policy*, *43*(3), 476–494.

Acs, Z. J., Stam, E., Audretsch, D. B., & O'Connor, A. (2017). 'The lineages of the entrepreneurial ecosystem approach'. *Small Business Economics*, *49*(1), 1–10.

Agrawal, A., Kapur, D., & McHale, J. (2008). 'How do spatial and social proximity influence knowledge flows? Evidence from patent data'. *Journal of Urban Economics*, *64*(2), 258–269.

Allaire, Y., & Firsirotu, M. E. (1984). 'Theories of organizational culture'. *Organization Studies*, *5*(3), 193–226.

Altintas, G., & Royer, I. (2009). 'Renforcement de la résilience par un apprentissage post-crise: une étude longitudinale sur deux périodes de turbulence'. *Mana Gement*, *12*(4), 266–293.

Amin, A., & Cohendet, P. (2004). *Architectures of knowledge: Firms, capabilities, and communities*. Oxford University Press, Oxford.

ANAC annual report: https://www.anticorruzione.it/-/relazione-annuale-2021 (last accessed July 13 2022).

Andersen, K. V. (2013). 'The problem of embeddedness revisited: Collaboration and market types'. *Research Policy*, *42*(1), 139–148.

Argyres, N., Bercovitz, J., & Zanarone, G. (2020). 'The role of relationship scope in sustaining relational contracts in interfirm networks'. *Strategic Management Journal*, *41*(2), 222–245.

Asheim, B. T., Smith, H. L., & Oughton, C. (2011). 'Regional innovation systems: Theory, empirics and policy'. *Regional Studies*, *45*(7), 875–891.

Audretsch, D. B., Cunningham, J. A., Kuratko, D. F., Lehmann, E. E., & Menter, M. (2019). 'Entrepreneurial ecosystems: Economic, technological, and societal impacts'. *The Journal of Technology Transfer*, *44*(2), 313–325.

Autant-Bernard, C. (2001). 'The geography of knowledge spillovers and technological proximity'. *Economics of Innovation and New Technology*, *10*(4), 237–254.

Autio, E., Kenney, M., Mustar, P., Siegel, D., & Wright, M. (2014). 'Entrepreneurial innovation: The importance of context'. *Research Policy*, *43*(7), 1097–1108.

Baccarani, C., Cassia, F., Rossato, C., & Cavallo, D. (2019). 'Territory, firms and value co-creation synergies'. *Journal of Place Management and Development*, *12*(2), 197–208.

Baghersad, M., & Zobel, C. W. (2022). 'Organizational resilience to disruption risks: Developing metrics and testing effectiveness of operational strategies'. *Risk Analysis*, *42*(3), 561–579.

Balkyte, A., & Tvaronavičiene, M. (2010). 'Perception of competitiveness in the context of sustainable development: Facets of "sustainable competitiveness"'. *Journal of Business Economics and Management*, *11*(2), 341–365.

Banerjee, S. (2019). 'Foreign direct investments: Examining the roles of democracy, corruption and judicial systems across countries'. *Journal of Applied Business and Economics*, *21*(6), 2–46.

Barasa, L. (2018). 'Corruption, transaction costs, and innovation in Africa'. *African Journal of Science, Technology, Innovation and Development*, *10*(7), 811–821.

Barile, S., & Saviano, M. (2018). Complexity and sustainability in management: Insights from a systems perspective. In *Social dynamics in a systems perspective* (pp. 39–63). Springer, Cham, New York.

Barnes-Mauthe, M., Oleson, K. L., Brander, L. M., Zafindrasilivonona, B., Oliver, T. A., & van Beukering, P. (2015). 'Social capital as an ecosystem service: Evidence from a locally managed marine area'. *Ecosystem Services*, *16*, 283–293

Baškarada, S., & Koronios, A. (2018). 'The 5S organizational agility framework: A dynamic capabilities perspective'. *International Journal of Organizational Analysis*, *26*(2), 331–342.

Basu, G. (2014). 'Concealment, corruption, and evasion: A transaction cost and case analysis of illicit supply chain activity'. *Journal of Transportation Security*, *7*(3), 209–226.

Baù, M., Chirico, F., Pittino, D., Backman, M., & Klaesson, J. (2019). 'Roots to grow: Family firms and local embeddedness in rural and urban contexts'. *Entrepreneurship Theory and Practice*, *43*(2), 360–385.

Becattini, G. (1987). Introduzione. Il Distretto Industriale Marshalliano: Cronaca di un Ritrovamento. In G. Becattini (Ed.), *Mercato e Forze Locali: Il Distretto industriale* (pp. 7–34). Il Mulino, Bologna.

Bedő, Z., Erdős, K., & Pittaway, L. (2020). 'University-centred entrepreneurial ecosystems in resource-constrained contexts'. *Journal of Small Business and Enterprise Development*, *27*(7), 1149–1166.

Bell, S. J., Tracey, P., & Heide, J. B. (2009). 'The organization of regional clusters'. *Academy of Management Review*, *34*(4), 623–642.

Berkes, F., & Ross, H. (2013). 'Community resilience: Toward an integrated approach'. *Society & Natural Resources*, *26*(1), 5–20.

Bertoncin, M., Faggi, P., Pase, A., & Quatrida, D. (2015). 'La prossimità: Una chiave geografica per interpretare i progetti di sviluppo'. *Territori Epigenetici*, *48*, 55–62.

Besharov, M. L., & Smith, W. K. (2014). 'Multiple institutional logics in organizations: Explaining their varied nature and implications'. *Academy of Management Review*, *39*(3), 364–381.

BGE. Instituto Brasileiro de Geografia e Estatística. Censos Demográficos de 2000–2020. https://www.ibge.gov.br/estatisticas/sociais/populacao/22827-censo-2020-censo4.html?=&t=destaques (last accessed July 2022).

Bologna, J. (2017). 'Corruption, product market competition, and institutional quality: Empirical evidence from the US states'. *Economic Inquiry*, *55*(1), 137–159.

Boschma, R. (2005). 'Proximity and innovation: A critical assessment'. *Regional Studies*, *39*(1), 61–74.

Bouba-Olga, O., Ferru, M., & Pépin, D. (2012). 'Exploring spatial features of science-industry partnerships: A study on French data'. *Papers in Regional Science*, *91*(2), 355–375.

Bowles, R., Faure, M., & Garoupa, N. (2000). 'Economic analysis of the removal of illegal gains'. *International Review of Law and Economics*, *20*(4), 537–549.

Brondizio, E. S., Ostrom, E., & Young, O. R. (2009). 'Connectivity and the governance of multilevel social-ecological systems: The role of social capital'. *Annual Review of Environment and Resources*, *34*, 253–278.

Brown, R., & Mason, C. (2017). 'Looking inside the spiky bits: A critical review and conceptualisation of entrepreneurial ecosystems'. *Small Business Economics*, *49*(1), 11–30.

Brunetta, G., Ceravolo, R., Barbieri, C. A., Borghini, A., de Carlo, F., Mela, A., & Voghera, A. (2019). 'Territorial resilience: Toward a proactive meaning for spatial planning'. *Sustainability*, *11*(8), 2286.

Burns, T., & Stalker, G. M. (1961). *The management of innovation*. Tavistock, London.

Calabrò, F. (2020). 'La programmazione integrata per la valorizzazione dei centri storici minori. Il Modello SOSTEC per la verifica della fattibilità economica per la valorizzazione degli immobili pubblici inutilizzati'. *ArcHistoR*, *7*(13), 1508–1523.

Calabrò, F., & Cassalia, G. (2017). Territorial cohesion: Evaluating the urban-rural linkage through the lens of public investments. In *International conference on smart and sustainable planning for cities and regions* (pp. 573–587). Springer, Cham, New York.

Capello, R. (1999). 'Spatial transfer of knowledge in high technology milieux: Learning versus collective learning processes'. *Regional studies*, *33*(4), 353–365.

Capello, R. (2009). 'Spatial spillovers and regional growth: A cognitive approach'. *European Planning Studies*, *17*(5), 639–658.

Capello, R. (2018). 'Cohesion policies and the creation of a European identity: The role of territorial identity'. *JCMS: Journal of Common Market Studies*, *56*(3), 489–503.

Capello R. (2019). 'Interpreting and understanding territorial identity'. *Regional Science Policy & Practice*, *11(1)*, 141-158.

Carayannis, E. G., Dezi, L., Gregori, G., & Calo, E. (2022). 'Smart environments and techno-centric and human-centric innovations for Industry and Society 5.0: A quintuple helix innovation system view towards smart, sustainable, and inclusive solutions'. *Journal of the Knowledge Economy*, *13*(2), 926–955.

Casson, M. C., Della Giusta, M., & Kambhampati, U. S. (2010). 'Formal and informal institutions and development'. *World Development*, *38*(2), 137–141.

Cavallo, A., Ghezzi, A., & Balocco, R. (2019). 'Entrepreneurial ecosystem research: Present debates and future directions'. *International Entrepreneurship and Management Journal*, *15*(4), 1291–1321.

Chen, Z., Fuller, D. B., & Zheng, L. (2018). 'Institutional isomorphism and Chinese private corporate philanthropy: State coercion, corruption, and other institutional effects'. *Asian Business & Management*, *17*(2), 83–111.

Choi, D. Y., & Gray, E. R. (2008). 'Socially responsible entrepreneurs: What do they do to create and build their companies?'. *Business Horizons*, *51*(4), 341–352.

Coase, R. E. (1988). 'The nature of the firm: Influence'. *Journal of Law, Economics, and Organization*, *4*, 33–48.

Cochrane, A. (2018). Relational thinking and the region. In A. Paasi, J. Harrison, & M. Jones (Eds.), *Handbook on the Geographies of Regions and Territories* (pp. 79–88). Edward Elgar Publishing, New York.

Colletis, G. (2010). 'Co-évolution des territoires et de la technologie: Une perspective institutionnaliste'. *Revue dEconomie Regionale Urbaine 2*, 235–249.

Córdova, R., Hogarth, N. J., & Kanninen, M. (2018). 'Sustainability of smallholder livelihoods in the ecuadorian highlands: A comparison of agroforestry and conventional agriculture systems in the indigenous territory of Kayambi People'. *Land*, *7*(2), 45.

Crevoisier, O. (2004). 'The innovative milieus approach: toward a territorialized understanding of the economy'?. *Economic Geography*, *80*(4), 367–379.

Crouch, C., Finegold, D., & Sako, M. (2001). *Are skills the answer?: The political economy of skill creation in advanced industrial countries*. Oxford University Press, Oxford.

Cuervo-Cazurra, A. (2016). 'Corruption in international business'. *Journal of World Business*, *51*(1), 35–49.

de las Heras-Rosas, C., & Herrera, J. (2020). 'Family firms and sustainability. A longitudinal analysis'. *Sustainability*, *12*(13), 5477.

Dekker, J., & Hasso, T. (2016). 'Environmental performance focus in private family firms: The role of social embeddedness'. *Journal of Business Ethics*, *136*(2), 293–309.

Del Baldo, M. (2012). 'Corporate social responsibility and corporate governance in Italian SMEs: The experience of some "spirited businesses"'. *Journal of Management & Governance*, *16*(1), 1–36.

Delgado, M., Porter, M. E., & Stern, S. (2010). 'Clusters and entrepreneurship'. *Journal of Economic Geography*, *10*(4), 495–518.

Della Porta, D., & Vannucci, A. (2016). *The hidden order of corruption: an institutional approach*. Routledge, Abingdon, Oxfordshire.

Dicken, P., & Malmberg, A. (2001). 'Firms in territories: a relational perspective'. *Economic Geography*, *77*(4), 345–363.

Dierkes, M., & Preston, L. E. (1977). 'Corporate social accounting reporting for the physical environment: A critical review and implementation proposal'. *Accounting, Organizations and Society*, *2*(1), 3–22.

DiMaggio, P. J., & Powell, W. W. (1983). 'The iron cage revisited: Institutional isomorphism and collective rationality in organizational fields'. *American Sociological Review*, *48*(2), 147–160.

Drees, J. M., & Heugens, P. P. (2013). 'Synthesizing and extending resource dependence theory: A meta-analysis'. *Journal of Management*, *39*(6), 1666–1698.

Duarte, A., Braga, V., Marques, C., & Sá, A. A. (2020). 'Geotourism and territorial development: A systematic literature review and research agenda'. *Geoheritage*, *12*(3), 1–19.

Dur, R., & Vollaard, B. (2019). 'Salience of law enforcement: A field experiment'. *Journal of Environmental Economics and Management*, *93*, 208–220.

Durand, R., & Thornton, P. H. (2018). 'Categorizing institutional logics, institutionalizing categories: A review of two literatures'. *Academy of Management Annals*, *12*(2), 631–658.

Dyer, J. H., & Singh, H. (1998). 'The relational view: Cooperative strategy and sources of interorganizational competitive advantage'. *Academy of Management Review*, *23*(4), 660–679.

El Talla, S. A., Al Shobaki, M. J., Abu-Naser, S. S., & Abu Amuna, Y. M. (2018). 'Organizational structure and its relation to the prevailing pattern of communication in palestinian universities', http://dstore.alazhar.edu.ps/xmlui/handle/123456789/379

Emerson, R. M. (2019). Power-dependence relations. In *Power in modern societies* (pp. 48–58). Routledge, Abingdon, Oxfordshire.

Feldman, M., Francis, J., & Bercovitz, J. (2005). 'Creating a cluster while building a firm: Entrepreneurs and the formation of industrial clusters'. *Regional Studies*, *39*(1), 129–141.

Feldman, M. P., & Zoller, T. D. (2016). Dealmakers in place: Social capital connections in regional entrepreneurial economies. *Handbook of Social Capital and Regional Development*. Edward Elgar, Cheltenham.

Filser, M., Kraus, S., Roig-Tierno, N., Kailer, N., & Fischer, U. (2019). 'Entrepreneurship as catalyst for sustainable development: Opening the black box'. *Sustainability*, *11*(16), 4503.

Fisman, R., Paravisini, D., & Vig, V. (2017). 'Cultural proximity and loan outcomes'. *American Economic Review*, *107*(2), 457–492.

Formisano, V., Quattrociocchi, B., Fedele, M., & Calabrese, M. (2018). 'From viability to sustainability: The contribution of the viable systems approach' (VSA). *Sustainability*, *10*(3), 725.

Foucault, M. (2007). *Security, territory, population: Lectures at the Collège de France, 1977–78*. Springer, New York.

Frigotto, M. L., Young, M., & Pinheiro, R. (2022). 'Resilience in organizations and societies: The state of the art and three organizing principles for moving forward'. *Towards Resilient Organizations and Societies*, 3–40.

Frynas, J. G., & Yamahaki, C. (2016). 'Corporate social responsibility: Review and roadmap of theoretical perspectives'. *Business Ethics: A European Review*, *25*(3), 258–285.

Furmankiewicz, M., Janc, K., & Macken-Walsh, Á. (2021). 'Implementation of the EU LEADER programme at member-state level: Written and unwritten rules of local project selection in rural Poland'. *Journal of Rural Studies*, *86*, 357–365.

Gaur, S. S., Bathula, H., & Singh, D. (2015). 'Ownership concentration, board characteristics and firm performance: A contingency framework'. *Management Decision*, *53*(5), 911–931.

Gibbs, D. (2009). 'Sustainability entrepreneurs, ecopreneurs and the development of a sustainable economy'. *Greener Management International*, *55*, 63–68.

Gilly, J. P., Kechidi, M., & Talbot, D. (2014). 'Resilience of organisations and territories: The role of pivot firms'. *European Management Journal*, *32*(4), 596–602.

Gilly, J. P., & Torre, A. (2000). *Dynamiques de proximité* (p. np). L'Harmattan.

Gkartzios, M., & Lowe, P. (2019). Revisiting neo-endogenous rural development. In *The Routledge Companion to Rural Planning* (pp. 159–169). Routledge, Abingdon, Oxfordshire.

Golinelli, G. M. (2013). 'Il CUEIM e Sinergie per lo sviluppo del territorio: Alcune note a margine (CUEIM and Sinergie for the development of territory, some notes)'. *Sinergie Italian Journal of Management*, *31*(Jan–Apr), 3–10.

Golinelli, G. M., & Bassano, C. (2012). Human resources for governing business dynamics. The viable systems approach. In J. C. Spohrer & L. Freund (Eds.), *Advances in the human side of service engineering* (pp. 359–368).

Gonçalves, E., Lemos, M. B., & Negri, J. A. D. (2011). 'The role of firm and territory in innovative activities in Brazilian post-opening economy'. *Economia Aplicada*, *15*, 103–130.

Gordon, G. G. (1991). 'Industry determinants of organizational culture'. *Academy of Management Review*, *16*(2), 396–415.

Governa, F., & Salone, C. (2004). 'Territories in action, territories for action: The territorial dimension of Italian local development policies'. *International Journal of Urban and Regional Research*, *28*(4), 796–818.

Grandori, A. (1997). 'An organizational assessment of interfirm coordination modes'. *Organization Studies*, *18*(6), 897–925.

Greenwood, M. J., & Tao, L. (2021). 'Regulatory monitoring and university financial reporting quality: Agency and resource dependency perspectives'. *Financial Accountability & Management*, *37*(2), 163–183.

Hage, J. & Aiken, M. (1967). 'Relationship of centralization to other structural properties'. *Administrative Science Quarterly*, *12*, 72–92.

Häkli, J., & Paasi, A. (2018). Geography, space and identity. In *Voices from the North* (pp. 141–155). Routledge, Abingdon, Oxfordshire.

Hanousek, J., Shamshur, A., Svejnar, J., & Tresl, J. (2021). 'Corruption level and uncertainty, FDI and domestic investment'. *Journal of International Business Studies*, *52*, 1750–1774.

Harhoff, D. (2000). 'R&D spillovers, technological proximity, and productivity growth—evidence from German panel data'. *Schmalenbach Business Review*, *52*(3), 238–260.

Hassink, R. (2005). 'How to unlock regional economies from path dependency? From learning region to learning cluster'. *European Planning Studies*, *13*(4), 521–535.

Hill, D. J., & Chen, G. (2006). Power systems as dynamic networks. In *2006 IEEE international symposium on circuits and systems (ISCAS)* (pp. 722-725). IEEE.

Hillman, A. J., Withers, M. C., & Collins, B. J. (2009). 'Resource dependence theory: A review'. *Journal of management*, *35*(6), 1404–1427.

Hinings, B., Gegenhuber, T., & Greenwood, R. (2018). 'Digital innovation and transformation: An institutional perspective'. *Information and Organization*, *28*(1), 52–61.

Hodgson, G. M. (2006). 'What are institutions?'. *Journal of Economic Issues*, *40*(1), 1–25.

Hofstede, G. (1980). *Culture's consequences: International differences in work-related values*. Sage, Beverly Hills, CA.

Holcombe, S., & Kemp, D. (2020). 'From pay-out to participation: Indigenous mining employment as local development?'. *Sustainable Development*, *28*(5), 1122–1135.

Ibodullaevich, K. K., & Bahromovna, T. D. (2020). 'Corruption: Concept, genesis, evolution and survival trend's'. *International Journal of Discourse on Innovation, Integration and Education*, *1*(5), 409–413.

Istat. (2020) Annual Report, https://www.istat.it/storage/rapporto-annuale/2020/Rapportoannuale2020.pdf (last accessed July 13, 2022).

Jackson, D. J. (2011). 'What is an innovation ecosystem?'. *National Science Foundation*, *1*(2), 1–13.

Jesmin, I., & Hui, H. (2012). 'A review of literature on contingency theory in managerial accounting'. *African Journal of Business Management*, *6*(15), 5159–5164.

Jiang, H., Jia, N., Bai, T., & Bruton, G. D. (2021). 'Cleaning house before hosting new guests: A political path dependence model of political connection adaptation in the aftermath of anticorruption shocks'. *Strategic Management Journal*, *42*(10), 1793–1821.

Kashner, J. B. (1990). 'Changing the corporate culture'. *New Directions for Higher Education*, *1990*(71), 19–28.

Kast, F. E., & Rosenzweig, J. E. (1972). 'General systems theory: Applications for organization and management'. *Academy of Management Journal*, *15*(4), 447–465.

Kato, K. Y. M., Delgado, N. G., & Romano, J. O. (2022). 'Territorial approach and rural development challenges: Governance, state and territorial markets'. *Sustainability*, *14*(12), 7105.

Kechidi, M., & Talbot, D. (2010). 'Institutions and coordination: What is the contribution of a proximity-based analysis? The case of Airbus and its relations with the subcontracting network'. *International Journal of Technology Management*, *50*(3/4), 285–299.

Kibler, E., Kautonen, T., & Fink, M. (2014). 'Regional social legitimacy of entrepreneurship: Implications for entrepreneurial intention and start-up behaviour'. *Regional Studies*, *48*(6), 995–1015.

Kingston, C., & Caballero, G. (2009). 'Comparing theories of institutional change'. *Journal of Institutional Economics*, *5*(2), 151–180.

Kleiner, G. B., & Karpinskaya, V. A. (2019). Transition of firms from the traditional to ecosystem form of business: The factor of transaction costs. In *Competitive Russia: Foresight model of economic and legal development in the digital age. International scientific conference in memory of Oleg Inshakov* (pp. 3–14). Springer, Cham, New York.

Knoben, J., & Oerlemans, L. A. (2006). 'Proximity and inter-organizational collaboration: A literature review'. *International Journal of Management Reviews*, *8*(2), 71–89.

Koroso, N. H., Zevenbergen, J. A., & Lengoiboni, M. (2019). 'Land institutions' credibility: Analyzing the role of complementary institutions'. *Land Use Policy*, *81*, 553–564.

Kryshtanovych, M., Dzanyy, R., Topalova, E., Tokhtarova, I., & Pirozhenko, N. (2020). 'Challengers to conceptual understanding of sustainable development regarding decentralization of power and responsibility in the conditions of the postmodern society'. *Postmodern Openings*, *11*(3), 257–268.

Kuckertz, A. (2019). 'Let's take the entrepreneurial ecosystem metaphor seriously!'. *Journal of Business Venturing Insights*, *11*, e00124.

Kummitha, H. R. (2020). 'Eco-entrepreneurs organizational attitude towards sustainable community ecotourism development'. *Deturope*, *12*(1), 85–101.

Kwarteng, A., & Aveh, F. (2018). 'Empirical examination of organizational culture on accounting information system and corporate performance: Evidence from a developing country perspective'. *Meditari Accountancy Research*, *26*(4), 675–698.

Labianca, M., Rubertis, S. D., Belliggiano, A., Salento, A., & Navarro, F. (2020). Social innovation, territorial capital and LEADER experiences in Andalusia (Spain) and in Molise (Italy). In *Neoendogenous development in European rural areas* (pp. 111–131). Springer, Cham, New York.

Lambsdorff, J. G., & Teksoz, S. U. (2004). Corrupt relational contracting. In *The New Institutional Economics of Corruption* (pp. 152–165). Routledge, Abingdon, Oxfordshire.

Lampel, J., Bhalla, A., & Jha, P. P. (2014). 'Does governance confer organisational resilience? Evidence from UK employee owned businesses'. *European Management Journal*, *32*(1), 66–72.

Lawrence, P. R., & Lorsch, J. W. (1967). 'Differentiation and integration in complex organizations'. *Administrative Science Quarterly*, *12*(1), 1–47.

Lesourne, J. (1976). 'The optimal growth of the firm in a growing environment'. *Journal of Economic Theory*, *13*(1), 118–137.

Lian, H., Li, H., & Ko, K. (2019). 'Market-led transactions and illegal land use: Evidence from China'. *Land Use Policy*, *84*, 12–20.

Linkov, I., & Trump, B. D. (2019). *The science and practice of resilience*. Springer International Publishing, Cham, New York.

Lucas, R. E. (1988). 'On the mechanics of economic development'. *Journal of Monetary Economics 22*, 3–42.

Lundquist, J. H., Anderton, D. L., & Yaukey, D. (2014). *Demography: The study of human population*. Waveland Press, Long Grove IL.

Lundvall, B. Å. (2007). 'National innovation systems—analytical concept and development tool'. *Industry and innovation*, *14*(1), 95–119.

Lussault, M. (2007). Habiter, Du Lieu Au Monde. Réflexions Géographiques Sur L'habitat Humain. In *Habiter, Le Propre De L'humain* (pp. 35–52). La Découverte, Paris.

Lysova, E. I., Allan, B. A., Dik, B. J., Duffy, R. D., & Steger, M. F. (2019). 'Fostering meaningful work in organizations: A multi-level review and integration'. *Journal of Vocational Behavior*, *110*, 374–389.

Maddaloni, D. (2016). 'Whatever happened to Italy?'The crisis of the Italian pattern of development in the era of globalization'. *Athens Journal of Social Sciences*, *3*(4), 299–319

Maddaloni, D., & Moffa, G. (2021). 'Not only for work: Italian migrants in the Athens area'. *International Migration*, *59*(4), 238–252.

Malecki, E. J. (2018a). 'Entrepreneurs, networks, and economic development: A review of recent research'. In *Reflections and extensions on key papers of the first twenty-five years of advances*, Emerald Publishing Limited, Bingley.

Malecki, E. J. (2018b). 'Entrepreneurship and entrepreneurial ecosystems'. *Geography Compass*, *12*(3), e12359.

Malmberg, A., & Maskell, P. (2002). 'The elusive concept of localization economies: Towards a knowledge-based theory of spatial clustering'. *Environment and Planning A: Economy and Space*, *34*(3), 429–449.

Malmberg, A., Sölvell, Ö., & Zander, I. (1996). 'Spatial clustering, local accumulation of knowledge and firm competitiveness'. *Geografiska Annaler: Series B, Human Geography*, *78*(2), 85–97.

Manimala, M. J., & Wasdani, K. P. (2015). *Entrepreneurial ecosystem*. Springer, New York.

March, J. G. (1962). 'The business firm as a political coalition'. *The Journal of Politics*, *24*(4), 662–678.

Marotta, D. (2007). *Human capital and university-industry linkage's role in fostering firm innovation: An empirical study of Chile and Colombia* (Vol. 4443). World Bank Publications.

Marshall, A. (1890). *Principles of economics*. Macmillan & Co, London and New York.

Maskell, P. (2001). 'The firm in economic geography'. *Economic Geography*, *77*(4), 329–344.

McPherson, C. M., & Sauder, M. (2013). 'Logics in action: Managing institutional complexity in a drug court'. *Administrative Science Quarterly*, *58*(2), 165–196.

Meeus, M., & Oerlemans, L. (2005). 'Innovation strategies, interactive learning and innovation networks'. *Innovation and Institutions*, 152–189, https://doi.org/10.4337/9781845426729

Meshram, S. A., & Rawani, A. M. (2019). 'Understanding entrepreneurial ecosystem'. *International Journal of Social Ecology and Sustainable Development (IJSESD)*, *10*(3), 103–115.

Meyer, K. E., & Xin, K. R. (2018). 'Managing talent in emerging economy multinationals: Integrating strategic management and human resource management'. *The International Journal of Human Resource Management*, *29*(11), 1827–1855.

Michler, J. D., & Wu, S. Y. (2020). 'Relational contracts in agriculture: Theory and evidence'. *Annual Review of Resource Economics*, *12*(1), 111–127.

Miles, S., & Ringham, K. (2019). 'The boundary of sustainability reporting: Evidence from the FTSE100'. *Accounting, Auditing & Accountability Journal*, *33*(2), 357–390.

Miller, D., & Le Breton-Miller, I. (2021). 'Family firms: A breed of extremes?'. *Entrepreneurship Theory and Practice*, *45*(4), 663–681.

Moir, L. (2001). 'What do we mean by corporate social responsibility?'. *Corporate Governance: The International Journal of Business in Society*, *1*(2), 16–22.

Motoyama, Y., & Watkins, K. K. (2014). 'Examining the connections within the startup ecosystem: A case study of St. Louis'. Louis Kauffman Foundation Research Series on City, Metro, and Regional Entrepreneurship.

Nelson, D. R., Adger, W. N., & Brown, K. (2007). 'Adaptation to environmental change: Contributions of a resilience framework'. *Annual Review of Environment and Resources*, *32*(1), 395–419.

Nicotra, M., Romano, M., Del Giudice, M., & Schillaci, C. E. (2018). 'The causal relation between entrepreneurial ecosystem and productive entrepreneurship: A measurement framework'. *The Journal of Technology Transfer*, *43*(3), 640–673.

Niyobuhungiro, R. V., & Schenck, C. J. (2021). 'The dynamics of indiscriminate/illegal dumping of waste in Fisantekraal, Cape Town, South Africa'. *Journal of Environmental Management*, *293*, 112954.

North, D. C. (1990). *Institutions, institutional change and economic performance*. Cambridge University Press, Cambridge.

Obrad, C., & Gherheș, V. (2018). 'A human resources perspective on responsible corporate behavior. Case study: The multinational companies in western Romania'. *Sustainability*, *10*(3), 726.

O'Connor, A., Stam, E., Sussan, F., & Audretsch, D. B. (2018). *Entrepreneurial ecosystems. Place-based transformations and transitions*. Springer, New York.

OECD. (1996). The knowledge-based economy. In *OECD, STI outlook*. OECD, Paris.

Okunev, I. Y. (2018). 'Territorial and spatial identity: New approach to the basic concepts'. *Comparative Politics Russia*, *9*(1), 18–25.

Ombi, N., Ambad, S. N. A., & Bujang, I. (2018). 'The effect of business development services on small medium enterprises (SMEs) performance'. *International Journal of Academic Research in Business and Social Sciences*, *8*(3), 117–130.

Onyokoko, I. O., & Onuoha, B. C. (2021). 'Organizational flexibility and corporate resilience of manufacturing firms in south-south, Nigeria'. *Research Journal of Management Practice*, *2782*, 7674.

Orlando, M. J. (2004). 'Measuring spillovers from industrial R&D: On the importance of geographic and technological proximity'. *RAND Journal of Economics*, *35*(4), 777–786.

Ostrom, E. (2009). 'A general framework for analyzing sustainability of social-ecological systems'. *Science*, *325*(5939), 419–422.

Oswin, N. (2020). 'An other geography'. *Dialogues in Human Geography*, *10*(1), 9–18.

Otley, D. (2016). 'The contingency theory of management accounting and control: 1980–2014'. *Management Accounting Research*, *31*, 45–62.

Owen-Smith, J., & Powell, W. W. (2004). 'Knowledge networks as channels and conduits: The effects of spillovers in the Boston biotechnology community'. *Organization Science*, *15*(1), 5–21.

Painter, J. (2010). 'Rethinking territory'. *Antipode*, *42*(5), 1090–1118.

Panzera, E. (2022). Cultural heritage and territorial identity: The economic consequences of their synergies. In *Cultural heritage and territorial identity* (pp. 145–172). Springer, Chaim, New York.

Park, S. (2020). 'Size matters: Toward a contingency theory of diversity effects on performance'. *Public Performance & Management Review*, *43*(2), 278–303.

Parrish, B. D., & Foxon, T. J. (2009). 'Sustainability entrepreneurship and equitable transitions to a low-carbon economy'. *Greener Management International*, *55*, 47–62.

Pathiranage, Y. L., Jayatilake, L. V., & Abeysekera, R. (2020). 'A literature review on organizational culture towards corporate performance'. *International Journal of Management, Accounting and Economics*, *7*(9), 522–544.

Pavolová, H., Bakalár, T., Kudelas, D., & Puškárová, P. (2019). 'Environmental and economic assessment of rainwater application in households'. *Journal of Cleaner Production*, *209*, 1119–1125.

Penrose, E. T. (1959). *The theory of the growth of the firm* (3rd edition, 1995). Oxford University Press, New York.

Pike, A., Dawley, S., & Tomaney, J. (2010). 'Resilience, adaptation and adaptability'. *Cambridge Journal of Regions, Economy and Society*, *3*(1), 59–70.

Pitelis, C. (2012). 'Clusters, entrepreneurial ecosystem co-creation, and appropriability: A conceptual framework'. *Industrial and Corporate Change*, *21*(6), 1359–1388.

Porter, M. E. (1990). 'The competitive advantage of notions'. *Harvard Business Review*, *73*, 91.

Porter, M. E. (1998). 'Clusters and the new economics of competition'. *Harvard Business Review*, *76*(6), 77–90.

Porter, M. E. (2000). 'Location, competition, and economic development: Local clusters in a global economy'. *Economic Development Quarterly*, *14*(1), 15–34.

Porter, M., & Ketels, C. (2009). Clusters and industrial districts: Common roots, different perspectives. In G. Becattini, M. Bellandi, & L. De Propis (Eds.), *A handbook of industrial districts*. Edward Elgar Publishing, New York.

Pred, A. (1966). 'Manufacturing in the American mercantile city: 1800–1840'. *Annals of the Association of American Geographers*, *56*(2), 307–338.

Preiser, R., Biggs, R., De Vos, A., & Folke, C. (2018). 'Social-ecological systems as complex adaptive systems'. *Ecology and Society*, *23*(4), 1–15.

Primdahl, J., Kristensen, L. S., Arler, F., Angelstam, P., Christensen, A. A., & Elbakidze, M. (2018). Rural landscape governance and expertise: On landscape agents and democracy. In *Defining Landscape Democracy*. Edward Elgar Publishing, New York.

Prokop, D. (2021). 'University entrepreneurial ecosystems and spinoff companies: Configurations, developments and outcomes'. *Technovation*, *107*, 102286.

Quimbayo Ruiz, G. A. (2020). 'Territory, sustainability, and beyond: Latin American urbanization through a political ecology'. *Environment and Planning E: Nature and Space*, *3*(3), 786–809.

Ramirez-Marquez, J. E., Rocco, C. M., Barker, K., & Moronta, J. (2018). 'Quantifying the resilience of community structures in networks'. *Reliability Engineering & System Safety*, *169*, 466–474.

Ravazzoli, E., Hoffman, C., Calabrò, F., & Cassalia, G. (2019). Rural–urban relationships for better territorial development. In *International conference on smart and sustainable planning for cities and regions* (pp. 557–565). Springer, Cham, New York.

Reyneri, E. (1998). 'The role of the underground economy in irregular migration to Italy: Cause or effect?'. *Journal of Ethnic and Migration Studies*, *24*(2), 313–331.

Rezaee, Z., Azar, A., Moghbel, A., & Dehghan Nayeri, M. (2018). 'Diagnosing organizational structure based on the viable system model (VSM)'. *Modern Research in Decision Making*, *3*(1), 187–215.

Risse, T. (2002). Transnational actors and world politics. In W. Carlsnaes, T. Risse, & B. A. Simmons (Eds.), *Handbook of international relations* (pp. 255–274). Sage, London.

Rodríguez-Pose, A. (2013). 'Do institutions matter for regional development'?. *Regional Studies*, *47*(7), 1034–1047.

Ruiz-Martin, C., Pérez Rios, J. M., Wainer, G., Pajares, J., Hernández, C., & López-Paredes, A. (2017). The application of the viable system model to enhance organizational resilience. In *Advances in Management Engineering* (pp. 95–107). Springer Cham, New York.

Ryszawska, B. (2018). Sustainable finance: Paradigm shift. In *Finance and Sustainability* (pp. 219–231). Springer Cham, New York.

Sassi, E., Benabdelhafid, A., & Hammami, S. (2019). 'Territory planning model integrating GIS and supply chain'. *International Journal of Transportation Engineering and Technology*, *6*(1), 1–15.

Schindler, S., & Kanai, J. M. (2021). 'Getting the territory right: Infrastructure-led development and the re-emergence of spatial planning strategies'. *Regional Studies*, *55*(1), 40–51.

Scott, W. R. (1995). 'Institutions and organizations. Ideas, interests and identities'. *Management*, *17*(2), 136–140.

Scott, W. R., & Davis, G. F. (2015). *Organizations and organizing: Rational, natural and open systems perspectives*. Routledge, Abingdon, Oxfordshire.

Shane, S., & Cable, D. (2002). 'Network ties, reputation, and the financing of new ventures'. *Management Science*, *48*(3), 364–381.

Sharafizad, J., Redmond, J., & Parker, C. (2022). 'The influence of local embeddedness on the economic, social, and environmental sustainability practices of regional small firms'. *Entrepreneurship & Regional Development*, *34*(1–2), 57–81.

Simeonova, V., Bos, E. J., Jongman, R. H. G., & Zingstra, H. L. (2009). *Implementation of ecological networks in different socio-economic contexts: Guiding principles based on experiences in Central and Eastern Europe* (No. 1896). Alterra.

Simone, C., Barile, S. (2016). '"Preface", special issue on environment, health and business management: linking efficiency and effectiveness to viable sustainability'. *International Journal of Environment and Health*, *7*(4), 5–6.

Simone, C., Barile, S., & Calabrese, M. (2018). 'Managing territory and its complexity: A decision-making model based on the viable system approach (VSA)'. *Land Use Policy*, *72*, 493–502.

Simone, C., Barondini, M. E., & Calabrese, M. (2015). 'Firm, territory and local community: Lessons learned from the Olivetti's model'. *Il Capitale Culturale. Studies on the Value of Cultural Heritage*, 7(4), 329–358.

Simone, C., Conti, M. E., & La Sala, A. (2019). 'Firm, territory and local community: Lessons learned from the Olivetti's model'. *Il Capitale Culturale. Studies on the Value of Cultural Heritage*, *20*, 403–428.

Simone, C., La Sala, A., & Montella, M. M. (2017). 'The rise of P2P ecosystem: A service logics amplifier for value co-creation'. *The TQM Journal*, *29*(6), 863–880.

Singh, S., Khare, A., Pandey, S. K., & Sharma, D. P. (2021). 'Industry and community peers as drivers of corporate social responsibility in India: The contingent role of institutional investors'. *Journal of Cleaner Production*, *295*, 126316.

Song, M., Ma, X., Zhao, X., & Zhang, L. (2022). 'How to enhance supply chain resilience: A logistics approach'. *The International Journal of Logistics Management*, (ahead-of-print).

Sorokin, P. A. (1942). Man and society in calamity, 1942; G. man and society in disaster, Transaction Publishers, New Brunswick.

Spigel, B. (2017). 'The relational organization of entrepreneurial ecosystems'. *Entrepreneurship Theory and Practice*, *41*(1), 49–72.

Spigel, B., & Harrison, R. (2018). 'Toward a process theory of entrepreneurial ecosystems'. *Strategic Entrepreneurship Journal*, *12*(1), 151–168.

Spilling, O. R. (1996). 'The entrepreneurial system: On entrepreneurship in the context of a megaevent'. *Journal of Business Research*, *36*(1), 91–103.

Sridharan, R., & Simatupang, T. M. (2013). 'Power and trust in supply chain collaboration'. *International Journal of Value Chain Management*, 7(1), 76–96.

Staber, U., & Sydow, J. (2002). 'Organizational adaptive capacity: A structuration perspective'. *Journal of Management Inquiry*, *11*(4), 408–424.

Stam, E., & Van de Ven, A. (2021). 'Entrepreneurial ecosystem elements'. *Small Business Economics*, *56*(2), 809–832.

Stam, F. C., & Spigel, B. (2016). 'Entrepreneurial ecosystems. USE discussion paper series', *16*(13), 1–15.

Sternberg, R. (2021). 'Entrepreneurship and geography—some thoughts about a complex relationship'. *The Annals of Regional Science*, 1–26, https://doi.org/10.1007/s00168-021-01091-w.

Tang, P., Feng, Y., Li, M., & Zhang, Y. (2021). 'Can the performance evaluation change from central government suppress illegal land use in local governments? A new interpretation of Chinese decentralisation'. *Land Use Policy*, *108*, 105578.

Taylor, M., & Asheim, B. (2001). 'The concept of the firm in economic geography'. *Economic Geography*, *77*(4), 315–328.

Teece, D., Peteraf, M., & Leih, S. (2016). 'Dynamic capabilities and organizational agility: Risk, uncertainty, and strategy in the innovation economy'. *California Management Review*, *58*(4), 13–35.

Thompson, J. D. (1967). *Organizations in action: Social science bases of administrative theory*. McGraw-Hill, New York.

Tilley, F., & Parrish, B. D. (2006). 'From poles to wholes: Facilitating an integrated approach to sustainable entrepreneurship'. *World Review of Entrepreneurship, Management and Sustainable Development*, 2(4), 281–294.

Torre, A., & Portafoglio, F. (2014). Introduzione. Il Ruolo Delle Relazioni di Prossimità Nei Processi di Sviluppo Regionale e Territoriale. In A. Torre & F. Wallet (Eds.), *Sviluppo Regionale e Relazioni di Prossimità, Nuovi Orizzonti Nella Scienza Regionale*. Edward Elgar, London.

Tortia, E., & Troisi, R. (2021). 'The resilience and adaptative strategies of Italian cooperatives during the COVID-19 pandemic'. *Форсайт*, *15*(4 (eng)), 78–88.

Troisi, R., & Alfano, G. (2019). 'Towns as safety organizational fields: An institutional framework in times of emergency'. *Sustainability*, *11*(24), 7025.

Troisi, R., & Alfano, G. (2021). 'Is regional emergency management key to containing COVID-19? A comparison between the regional Italian models of Emilia-Romagna and Veneto'. *International Journal of Public Sector Management*, *35*(2), 195–210.

Troisi, R., & Alfano, G. (2022a). 'The re-election of corrupt mayors: Context, relational leadership and level of corruption'. *Local Government Studies*, 1–22, https://doi.org/10.1080/03003930.2022.2087060

Troisi, R., & Alfano, G. (2022b). 'Proximity and inter-firm corruption: A transaction cost approach'. *Small Business Economics*, 1–16, https://doi.org/10.1007/s11187-022-00649-y

Troisi, R., Di Nauta, P., & Piciocchi, P. (2021). 'Private corruption: An integrated organizational model'. *European Management Review*, https://doi.org/10.1111/emre.12489

Ucar, E. (2018). 'Local creative culture and corporate innovation'. *Journal of Business Research*, *91*, 60–70.

Ufere, N., Gaskin, J., Perelli, S., Somers, A., & Boland, Jr, R. (2020). 'Why is bribery pervasive among firms in sub-Saharan African countries? Multi-industry empirical evidence of organizational isomorphism'. *Journal of Business Research*, *108*, 92–104.

Utterback, J. M. (1974). 'Innovation in industry and the diffusion of technology'. *Science*, *183*(4125), 620–626.

Valdaliso, J. M., & Wilson, J. R. (Eds.). (2015). *Strategies for shaping territorial competitiveness*. Routledge, Oxford.

Van der Waal, J. W., & Thijssens, T. (2020). 'Corporate involvement in sustainable development goals: Exploring the territory'. *Journal of Cleaner Production*, *252*, 119625.

Van Hauwaert, S. M., Schimpf, C. H., & Dandoy, R. (2019). 'Populist demand, economic development and regional identity across nine European countries: Exploring regional patterns of variance'. *European Societies*, *21*(2), 303–325.

van Winden, F. A., & Ash, E. (2012). 'On the behavioral economics of crime'. *Review of Law & Economics*, *8*(1), 181–213.

Vargo, S. L., Wieland, H., & Akaka, M. A. (2015). 'Innovation through institutionalization: A service ecosystems perspective'. *Industrial Marketing Management*, *44*, 63–72.

Venard, B. (2009). 'Organizational isomorphism and corruption: An empirical research in Russia'. *Journal of Business Ethics*, *89*(1), 59–76.

Verdu, A. J., & Gómez-Gras, J. M. (2009). 'Measuring the organizational responsiveness through managerial flexibility'. *Journal of Organizational Change Management*, *22*(6), 668–690.

Vogus, T. J., & Sutcliffe, K. M. (2007). Organizational resilience: Towards a theory and research agenda. In *2007 IEEE international conference on systems, man and cybernetics* (pp. 3418–3422). IEEE.

Wei, Z., Shen, H., Zhou, K. Z., & Li, J. J. (2017). 'How does environmental corporate social responsibility matter in a dysfunctional institutional environment? Evidence from China'. *Journal of Business Ethics*, *140*(2), 209–223.

Weick, K. E. (1969). *The social psychology of organizing*. Addison-Wesley, Reading, MA.

Weick, K. E., & Sutcliffe, K. M. (2007). *Managing the unexpected: Resilient performance in and age of uncertainty* (2nd edition). Jossey-Bass, San Francisco, CA.

Wilkesmann, M., & Wilkesmann, U. (2018). 'Industry 4.0–organizing routines or innovations?'. *VINE Journal of Information and Knowledge Management Systems*, *48*(2), 238–254.

Williamson, O. E. (1996). *The mechanisms of governance*. Oxford University Press, Oxford.

Williamson, O. E. (2008). 'Outsourcing: Transaction cost economics and supply chain management'. *Journal of Supply Chain Management*, *44*(2), 5–16.

Woolley, J. L., Pozner, J. E., & DeSoucey, M. (2022). 'Raising the bar: Values-driven niche creation in US bean-to-bar chocolate'. *Strategy Science*, *7*(1), 27–55.

World Commission on Environment and Development. (1987). *Our common future*. Oxford University Press, Oxford.

Yasai-Ardekani, M. (1989). 'Effects of environmental scarcity and munificence on the relationship of context to organizational structure'. *Academy of Management Journal*, *32*(1), 131–156.

You, H., Zhang, J., & Song, Y. (2022). 'Assessing conflict of farmland institutions using credibility theory: Implications for socially acceptable land use'. *Land Use Policy*, *112*, 105817.

Zamagni, S. (2008). 'Reciprocity, civil economy, common good'. In *Pursuing the common good: How solidarity and subsidiarity can work together* (pp. 467–502), Pontifical Academy of Social Sciences, Rome, Vatican City.

Zeller, C. (2004). 'North Atlantic innovative relations of Swiss pharmaceuticals and the proximities with regional biotech arenas'. *Economic Geography*, *80*(1), 83–111.

Zhao, H., Teng, H., & Wu, Q. (2018). 'The effect of corporate culture on firm performance: Evidence from China'. *China Journal of Accounting Research*, *11*(1), 1–19.

Zimmermann, J. B. (2001). 'The firm/territory relationships in the globalisation: Towards a new rationale'. *European Journal of Economic and Social Systems*, *15*(1), 57–75.

Acknowledgements

I'd like to thank the following individuals for their assistance with this project: Gaetano Alfano for the exchange of ideas that allowed me to see things from a different perspective; William Bromwich and Mohammad Zarei for extensive English editing; and Luigi Valanzano for the map in Chapter 3.

Index

Page numbers in *Italic* refer to figures; and in **Bold** refer to tables.